Instructor's Resource Manual with Core Concept Video Instructor's Guide

to accompany

LIBERTY EQUALITY POWER

A History of the American People

Third Edition

Volume I: To 1877

John M. Murrin
Princeton University

Paul E. Johnson
University of South Carolina

James M. McPherson
Princeton University

Gary Gerstle
University of Maryland

Emily S. Rosenberg
Macalester College

Norman L. Rosenberg
Macalester College

Prepared by
Janet G. Brantley
Texarkana College

WADSWORTH

THOMSON LEARNING

Australia   Canada   Mexico   Singapore   Spain   United Kingdom   United States

Printed in the United States of America

1 2 3 4 5 6 7   05 04 03 02 01

0-15-506058-9

Cover credit: *North American Medicine Pipe Stem Dance* by Paul Kane (1810–71). Bridgeman Art Library/ SuperStock.

For more information about our products, contact us at:
Thomson Learning Academic Resource Center
1-800-423-0563

For permission to use material from this text, contact us by:
Phone: 1-800-730-2214
Fax: 1-800-730-2215
Web: www.thomsonrights.com

Asia
Thomson Learning
60 Albert Complex, #15-01
Albert Complex
Singapore 189969

Australia
Nelson Thomson Learning
102 Dodds Street
South Melbourne, Victoria 3205
Australia

Canada
Nelson Thomson Learning
1120 Birchmount Road
Toronto, Ontario M1K 5G4
Canada

Europe/Middle East/South Africa
Thomson Learning
Berkshire House
168-173 High Holborn
London WC1 V7AA
United Kingdom

Latin America
Thomson Learning
Seneca, 53
Colonia Polanco
11560 Mexico D.F.
Mexico

Spain
Paraninfo Thomson Learning
Calle/Magallanes, 25
28015 Madrid, Spain

PREFACE

This Instructor's Resource Manual is intended as a teaching supplement. It is designed to accompany Harcourt's *Liberty, Equality, Power: A History of the American People*, Third Edition. In this manual's revision, I have attempted to augment the innovative thematic approach used by the textbook's authors. I have retained the basic format of earlier editions of the manual, including the "Liberty, Equality, Power: A Thematic Braid" section. It is my hope that instructors will consider this manual a useful resource that will complement what I consider to be a well-balanced, lively, and insightful narrative of the American experience.

The author of the Instructor's Resource Manual has extensive experience in teaching American history. This manual is not intended to instruct instructors in how to teach history. Rather, it is assumed that those adopting the *Liberty, Equality, Power* text have done advanced work in American history or are in the process of doing so. However, it has been my experience that a large number of survey classes are taught by graduate students or adjunct faculty. Such instructors sometimes feel almost overwhelmed by the multiple tasks of teaching well while deciding what aspect of their instruction needs the greatest emphasis. I hope that the Instructor's Resource Manual will assist these less experienced instructors while still proving beneficial to those who have taught more extensively. It should help instructors plan their classes and develop quality assignments based closely on the textbook material, while at the same time serving as a worthwhile guide to the material contained in the text itself. I feel confident that instructors consulting the manual will see a direct correlation between manual and textbook.

The Instructor's Resource Manual consists of separate sections, including a chapter summary, a list of identification terms, a chronology, suggested thematic topics for classroom discussion and written assignments, geography objectives, and a brief guide to video resources to augment classroom lectures. The extensive chapter outlines have been heavily revised for the Third Edition. A new feature to this manual is the Suggested Web Activities for the Classroom section. The textbook authors have incorporated Web sites into the Third Edition, and the publisher's Web page contains numerous links and activities pertinent to each chapter. In the manual's Web Activity section, I have included some rather unique sites, chosen for their adaptability to *classroom* use. I suggest accessing these sites via the Internet with a large screen for classroom viewing and discussion. I have included ideas on how they can best be utilized without taking up too much valuable class time. The sites were chosen for their ability to enlighten students through a "you are there" type of experience.

Liberty, Equality, Power: A History of the American People is an exceptional college textbook—in part because of its unique thematic concept and the consistency with which that theme is applied. To maintain that consistency, the "Thematic Braid" portion of the manual encapsulates the major overall themes of each chapter, summarizing the text authors' skillful interweaving of the themes of liberty, equality, and power.

We, as instructors of American history, come to the discipline from various backgrounds and with sometimes widely varying needs. It is therefore impossible to construct one manual that will meet all instructors' requirements. I believe that the original authors of this manual have laid down an effective framework that I hope I have only improved upon in this revision. I trust that all instructors will find it a useful resource for teaching with *Liberty, Equality, Power: A History of the American People*, Third Edition.

Janet G. Brantley

CONTENTS

Chapter 1

WHEN OLD WORLDS COLLIDE: CONTACT, CONQUEST, CATASTROPHE

CHAPTER SUMMARY

Most textbooks assume that "real" history did not begin in the Americas until after Europeans arrived in 1492. This chapter shows that a varied and complex past shaped Indian cultures and profoundly conditioned their response to the arrival of Europeans. Religious choices, gender relations, warfare, and trade differed enormously and created different value systems on the two sides of the Atlantic.

Christopher Columbus was far from being the first person to travel between the Eastern and Western Hemispheres. The first inhabitants of the Americas traversed the Beringia land bridge from Asia. Norsemen from Scandinavia sailed west across the North Atlantic long before 1492. The significance of Columbus's feat proved to be the permanent connection he inaugurated between the peoples, flora, and fauna of both sides of the Atlantic that had been separated for over 5,000 years. Called by historians the Columbian Exchange, this linking of East and West proved revolutionary for everyone and everything in Europe, Africa, North America, and South America.

No group suffered more from the Columbian Exchange than the Amerindian peoples, who had no immunity to smallpox and the other micro-parasites of the Europeans. The Inca and Aztec civilizations, so remarkable for their urban societies, native art and animistic religion, were no match for the armored and mounted Spanish forces, especially while suffering under the all-but-incalculable strain of virgin-soil epidemics. Within a few decades the great Amerindian civilizations all but disappeared. While Spanish and other European missionaries sought to do the work of God, their efforts failed to halt the brutal, inhuman treatment of the indigenous peoples of the Americas.

As a result of their exploration and conquest, Europeans—Iberians in particular—transformed themselves from a relatively weak and isolated region into the world's dominant civilization. In spite of brutal disregard for human life, huge bureaucratic inefficiency, and frequent internecine wars, the Europeans rode their warships in search of gold, glory, and the new places to spread the Gospel. In doing so, they marched toward world domination.

LIBERTY, EQUALITY, POWER: A THEMATIC BRAID

Columbus's voyage and those that followed were fueled in no small measure by the European desire for power, particularly the power to dominate eastern trade. European notions of equality, like those of the scattered civilizations of the globe, proved exceedingly limited. Indeed, the world in 1500 was one so full of hierarchy and inequality that virtually no one proposed, or even imagined, a society in which "all men are created equal." Indeed, the primary tenet of virtually all peoples proved to be the distinction between "us and them," a distinction that contributed to the ruthless and barbaric nature of the Columbian Exchange.

Cultural differences contributed to the Europeans' savage conquest of the Amerindian peoples. Missionary work and mass conversions failed to ease the effects of European domination and at times even abetted it. Far more important proved to be Europe's insatiable appetite for glory and wealth. The discovery of the vast and, for the most part, indefensible riches of the New World brought out the most aggressive traits in the conquerors. The dominant theme of European world conquest proved to be the search for wealth and power.

IDENTIFICATIONS

Beringia	Clovis tip
Norseman	Vinland
Inuit	Black Death
Johann Gutenberg	caravel
Islam	Prince Henry
Cape of Good Hope	Ferdinand and Isabella
Treaty of Tordesillas	Christopher Columbus
Ponce de León	Tenochtitlán
Cahokia	kiva
Anasazi	mound builders
Aztec	Maya
Hernán Cortés	slash and burn
Moctezuma	Inca
conquistadores	encomienda
haciendas	de Soto
Cabeza de Vaca	Coronado
Francisco Pizarro	Council of the Indies
smallpox	Columbian Exchange
Fray Bartolomé de Las Casas	Jesuits
Franciscans	Brazil

CHRONOLOGY

50,000–10,000 B.C.	Migrations over Beringia into the Americas.
9000–8000 B.C.	Clovis tip hunter-gatherer culture spreads throughout North America.
3400 B.C.–A.D. 700	Louisiana mound builders' culture extends through southeastern North America.
500 B.C.–A.D. 400	Adena-Hopewell mound builders flourish in the Ohio Valley.
A.D. 900–1200	Anasazi culture expands through southwest North America.
1001–1014	Leif Erikson leads three voyages to North America.
1347–1351	Bubonic plague, the "Black Death," decimates one third of the European population.
1400–1450	Aztec and Inca conquests of, respectively, Mesoamerica and Andean South America.
1434	Gil Eannes rounds Cape Bojador and returns safely to Portugal.
1430s	Johann Gutenberg invents movable-type printing press.
1440s	Portuguese enter the African slave trade.
	Spanish victory at Granada results in overthrow of last outpost of Islam in Iberia.
	Christopher Columbus's first voyage to the Western Hemisphere.
1494	Treaty of Tordesillas divides non-Christian world between Spanish and Portuguese.

© 2002 Thomson Learning, Inc.

1497–1499	Vasco da Gama sails to India and back.
1500	Portuguese discover Brazil.
1501	First slaves carried from Africa to the Americas.
1519	Ferdinand Magellan sets sail from Seville, Spain, beginning the first circumnavigation of the globe.
	Hernán Cortés begins conquest of Aztecs.
1528–1536	Cabeza de Vaca travels overland from Florida to Mexico.
1531–1532	Francisco Pizarro leads expedition against the Inca.
1539–1543	Hernando de Soto's expedition through the southeastern part of North America.
1540–1542	Francisco Vásquez de Coronado's expedition through the southwestern part of North America.
1540s	Spanish assume control over the silver mines at Potosí.
1570–1571	First Spanish Jesuit mission in Chesapeake Bay.
1580	Philip II unites the Spanish and Portuguese empires.

THEMATIC TOPICS FOR ENRICHMENT

1. What elements of world geography did Columbus possess knowledge of right before setting out in 1492? What elements did he have wrong?

2. Give examples of the biological, environmental, and cultural consequences of the Columbian Exchange.

3. Discuss the use of the word *catastrophe* to describe the results of "Old Worlds Colliding" in the fifteenth and sixteenth centuries.

4. List the merits and detractions of the following terms used to identify the peoples of the Americas: Indians, Americans, Amerindians, Natives, Native Americans.

5. Compare and contrast the various peoples who came to the Americas before 1600. Why did some stay while others did not?

6. Explain the statement: "In 1400, Europe stood at the edge, not the center, of world commerce."

7. Discuss the rise of Portugal as a seaborne empire in the fifteenth century. Why does the text call it an "unlikely pioneer"?

8. What were Columbus's motives in 1492, and what were those of the Spaniards who followed him to the Americas?

9. How did the Spanish conquistadores manage to subdue the great Amerindian civilizations of the Aztecs and the Incas?

10. Contrast the idealism and chauvinism of the missionary efforts in the Western Hemisphere.

GEOGRAPHY OBJECTIVES

1. Find the location of the following civilizations on a map: Mali, Chinese, Ottoman, Western European, Amerindian (pp. 9, 41).

2. Trace the route of the Silk Road. Show how Columbus intended to sail west to establish a competing trade route (p. 9).

3. Sketch where the Beringia land bridge was located when revealed by the lowered sea level of the last Ice Age (p. 4).

4. Locate the Maya, Aztec, Inca, Anasazi, and eastern woodlands peoples on a map of the Americas (p. 36).

5. Find Greenland, Alaska, and Tierra del Fuego on a map of the Western Hemisphere (p. 41).

SUGGESTED ESSAY TOPICS

1. Over the past 500 years, how has our evaluation of Columbus's voyages changed?

2. What advantages did Europeans have over other civilizations in 1500? What disadvantages did they turn to their ultimate benefit?

3. Create your own accounts of the conquest of the Aztec civilization from the contrasting points of view of Moctezuma and Cortés. In what ways can the conflict be described as a "cultural misunderstanding"?

4. What were the basic mechanisms of the slave trade? Assess the relationship of slavery to the conquest of the Western Hemisphere.

SUGGESTED WEB ACTIVITY FOR THE CLASSROOM

The Chetro Ketl Great Kiva: A Three-Dimensional Model

http://sipapu.ucsb.edu/great.kiva/old/index.html

Take students on a virtual tour of the Chetro Ketl Great Kiva at Chaco Canyon, New Mexico. Web site includes interactive rooms whose clickable items serve as teaching tools while entertaining visitors.

LECTURE OUTLINE

1. The story of the settlement of the Americas is only one part of a larger epic of **peoples in motion,** in which the Western Hemisphere was only one destination.

    a. The first immigrants traveled **from Beringia to the Americas** over the land bridge created during the last Ice Age.

        (Show Transparency 01-02: Map, Indian Settlement of America)

    b. Climatic changes led to the **great extinction** of the large mammals upon which the bands of hunters depended; extinction led to the **rise of agriculture** in the aftermath of the last Ice Age.

    c. Southeast Asian explorers known as **Polynesians** settled **Hawaii** and other islands in the eastern Pacific Ocean.

    d. Peoples from the north, **Norsemen,** traveled from the upper reaches of Europe to North America long before Columbus's voyages but left no permanent mark on the continent.

2. **Europe in the fifteenth century** was only a small part of a world that encompassed myriad complex and competing societies.

    a. For reasons that are not entirely clear, **China,** the world's most populous country and in many ways its most advanced, **rejected** any organized plan of **Overseas Expansion.**

b. One key theme of fifteenth-century expansion was the persistent conflict between **Europe and Islam,** a conflict complicated by the fact that both regions wanted to trade with each other even as they both feared increased interaction.

c. The **legacy of the Crusades,** which took place in the eleventh and twelfth centuries, was bitter enmity between Christians and Muslims, and also the European enslavement of large numbers of peoples from various lands.

d. **Portugal** was the **unlikely pioneer** of European expansion, as the nation of only several hundred thousand established a remarkable empire in Africa, India, and Asia.

e. Portugal's **exploration and colonization of Africa**'s western coast brought the African **slave trade** to Europeans in a virulent new form.

f. By the early 1500s, **Portugal's Asian empire** was bringing untold wealth to its people through trade, mainly in exotic spices.

g. The Portuguese capitalized on **early lessons** learned from others by improving both financial and maritime skills; others would in turn improve upon their knowledge, the result being an overall increase in the drive to succeed.

(Show Transparency 01-03: Map, Africa and the Mediterranean in the Fifteenth Century)

3. Much larger and more populous than its neighbor, **Spain** followed closely on Portugal's heels and soon eclipsed it in the race for **an Atlantic empire,** most notably under the combined leadership of Ferdinand and Isabella.

a. Sailing under the Spanish flag, Christopher **Columbus** accidentally found the Americas.

(Show Transparency 01-04: Map, Columbus's First Voyage, 1492)

b. In the aftermath of Columbus's expeditions, **Spain** quickly established an empire in **the Caribbean,** where the native "Indians" succumbed to overwork and disease, and were soon replaced by African slaves.

4. The centuries before European arrival witnessed the **emergence of complex societies in the Americas.**

a. The **rise of sedentary cultures** occurred throughout the Americas as agricultural transformation occurred.

   i. Along with the settlement into at least semi-sedentary lifestyles came large **population surges.**

   ii. The Indians remained a **largely Stone Age** society, although **some metal working** for ornamental purposes did occur.

b. The **Andes** contained a number of **cycles of complex cultures,** with the parent culture of the Olmecs arising along the Gulf Coast and Mayan culture dominating the lowlands of the Yucatán.

c. **Inca civilization** controlled the Andean realm for a short period around 1400 A.D.

d. Warriors from the North, the Aztecs, built a great culture centered on the capital city of **Tenochtitlán.**

(Show Transparency 01-05: Map, Ancient Mesoamerica)

e. **North American mound builders** dominated the eastern part of the continent and traded from coast to coast.

f. The Anasazi dominated **urban cultures of the Southwest.**

5. The year 1492 marked the first permanent **contact;** shortly thereafter, **cultural misunderstandings,** particularly over issues of religion and gender, resulted in conflict and open warfare.

6. By the turn of the century, cultural misunderstandings resulted in **conquest and catastrophe.**

    a. Hernán Cortés led a band of less than a thousand men in the **conquest of Mexico,** while little more than a decade later the **Pizarro brothers** brutally subdued the Incas in Peru.

    b. **North American conquistadores and missionaries** soon spread out from the Caribbean, simultaneously spreading Christianity and establishing Spanish dominion.

    (Show Transparency 01-06: Map, Principal Spanish Explorations of North America; and Transparency 01-07: Map, Spanish Missions in Florida and New Mexico, circa 1675)

    c. Through the sixteenth century, the **Spaniards** erected a remarkable **Empire** while unleashing a **demographic catastrophe** on the Indians.

    (Show Transparency 01-01: Aztec drawing, Smallpox Devastation in Peru, 1524)

    d. Spanish and other European seamen copied Portuguese activities in **Brazil,** creating the beginnings of a **global economy** based largely upon slave labor and staple crop production.

7. Historians have suggested many conflicting **explanations** for the various **patterns of conquest, submission, and resistance** in the century following Columbus's voyages.

Conclusion: By accident, on October 12, 1492, Christopher Columbus found America. From then on, and for the next several hundred years, Europeans contested for domination of the Western Hemisphere. The costs were high, and the consequences for the peoples of Europe, Africa, and the Americas proved all but immeasurable. For the indigenous peoples of the Western Hemisphere, the consequences of contact proved catastrophic.

FOCUS ON FEATURES

American Album: Global Empire and The Aesthetics of Power, p. 18
History Through Film: *The Mission,* p. 38
Link to the Past: Pictorial Images of the Transatlantic Slave Trade, p. 11

TEACHING RESOURCES

Vikings! is a nine-part series "through the legendary world" of the Norsemen, narrated by Magnus Magnusson. PBS Video (running time is about 60 minutes per tape).

Vikings in North America offers a briefer account of the early expeditions. A&E (50 minutes).

Surviving Columbus: The Story of the Pueblo People tells "the other side of history—as viewed by America's Pueblo people." PBS Home Video (52 minutes).

The First Americans reviews likely migration across Beringia into the Americas and is based on meteorological and archaeological evidence. Filmic Archives (53 minutes).

Mesa Verde National Park is an archaeological exploration through this Colorado national park, featuring Robert H. Lister, one of the United States's foremost anthropologists of the Anasazi civilization. Holiday Video Library (60 minutes).

The Ancient Ones, part of the Mystic Lands series, presents the spiritual story of the Anasazi, as told by Edward James Olmos. The Learning Channel/Discovery (22 minutes).

Ferdinand and Isabella tells the story of the Spanish monarchy in the age of Columbus. Filmic Archives (30 minutes).

Central America: The Burden of Time explores the ways the Aztecs and Mayas developed civilization isolated from the rest of the world. Filmic Archives (60 minutes).

The Search for Ancient Americans attempts to unlock the secrets of the American past through the examination of five archeological landmarks. Filmic Archives (58 minutes).

Ancestors takes a look at early North American cultures, including Kahokia, "the largest city in the U.S. before 1800." Warner Home Video (49 minutes).

Cannibals! examines missionary tales of human sacrifice and consumption in light of European bias and the historical record. Were the tales of cannibalism fantasy or fact? Films for the Humanities (28 minutes).

The Shape of the World: Staking a Claim details the Spanish conquistadores as they wreaked havoc upon the Mesoamerican and South American civilizations. Filmic Archives (55 minutes).

Ten Who Dared: Francisco Pizarro recreates this Spaniard's dramatic expedition of discovery and conquest. BBC/Time-Life Video (52 minutes).

Mysteries of Peru: Enigma of the Ruins explores in detail the remarkable and sophisticated Inca civilization of the Andes. Filmic Archives (50 minutes).

Chapter 2

THE CHALLENGE TO SPAIN
AND THE SETTLEMENT
OF NORTH AMERICA

CHAPTER SUMMARY

The tremendous booty the Spanish hauled back from the Americas inevitably led other European nations to challenge Spain in the New World. By the beginning of the seventeenth century, the Dutch, English, and French had staked their own claims to the Atlantic sea lanes, to the slave trade, and to lands in the Caribbean and in North America. Catholic New France, Protestant New Netherland, and the fledgling English colonies joined New Spain as outposts of the European empires.

The societies that these European nations created in the Western Hemisphere differed greatly from one another. They reflected the demographic, economic, and cultural features of their parent countries and yet proved remarkably distinctive in their own right. Like the motives of the Spanish conquistadores and hidalgos, those of the later settlers varied greatly. The earliest navigators—Cabot, Verrazzano, and Hudson—proved predominantly to be adventurers and explorers who, like Columbus, sought to gain quick riches through exploration and conquest. While many early settlers were impelled by the hope of gaining great wealth and personal fame, others sought to come to the West for religious and political reasons. The Protestant Reformation shook many of Europe's oldest institutions. Powerful Protestant movements in France, the Netherlands, and England challenged Catholicism in Europe. Similarly, Protestants sought to overturn Catholic Spain's domination of the Western Hemisphere. Finding no great societies like the Aztec or Inca that could be plundered, France, England, and the Netherlands gained little from their explorations through the first decades of the seventeenth century.

The French colonization effort centered in the Saint Lawrence River Valley, which Jacques Cartier had explored between 1534 and 1543. The inhabitants of New France established good relations with the indigenous tribes, with whom they engaged in a lucrative fur trade. Despite numerous hardships, including rather small numbers, extremely harsh winters, and the frequent indifference of the French crown, the missionaries and fur traders managed to establish a stable and successful, if not thriving, outpost in North America by the 1660s.

The Dutch settlement of North America, orchestrated by the Dutch West India Company, proved similar to that of the French. Establishing New Netherland primarily in the Hudson River Valley, the West India Company suffered from a lack of funds as well as a shortage of settlers. Even with the enticement of huge patroonships, the company simply could not attract enough settlers to become more than a trading entrepôt, with outposts on the island of Manhattan and at Fort Orange. Good relations with the Iroquois nation and a policy of toleration modeled on that of the home country, along with the efforts of zealous Dutch Reformed churchmen, enabled the colony to grow gradually through the first half of the seventeenth century.

England's early attempts to rival the Spanish failed for the most part. Only after their defeat of the Spanish Armada in 1588 and the union of West Country experience and London capital did British colonization of North America and the Caribbean become feasible.

The Virginia Company and the Massachusetts Bay Company, both joint-stock companies, and a small band of Protestant Separatists who landed at Plymouth in 1620 established the first permanent English colonies in North America. All three suffered from a lack of funds, harsh initial conditions, and strained relations with the Amerindian nations. Yet their experiences proved vastly different. The Puritan settlements in New England quickly developed into remarkably stable and secure colonies with a rapidly growing population and diverse economies. The Chesapeake colonies of Virginia and Maryland suffered from disease, warfare, and the boom-and-bust cycle of an economy based solely on tobacco production. Not until the middle of the seventeenth century did the Chesapeake colonies become a tolerably stable society of planters, indentured servants, and a growing number of African slaves.

After the restoration of the Stuart monarchy, England began a concerted effort to settle North America. Under Charles II, England founded several colonies. Charles made effective use of the colonies to help pay off debts, granting huge tracts of land, called proprietorships, in North America. By royal charter, Lord Ashley-Cooper established Carolina; the duke of York, the king's brother, transformed New Netherland into New York; Lords Carteret and Berkeley founded New Jersey; and William Penn created a Quaker refuge that the king called Pennsylvania.

In sum, then, the nations of northwestern Europe established a wide spectrum of settlements in the Americas. Although they differed greatly from one another, they were similar in the direct and enduring challenge they presented to Spanish dominance of the New World. At a fairly early date, England began to dominate in the area of true colonization.

LIBERTY, EQUALITY, POWER: A THEMATIC BRAID

European competition and conflict formed the backdrop of New World settlement in the sixteenth and seventeenth centuries. Conflict in Europe over power, religion, and empire spread inevitably into the Atlantic frontier, where England, France, and the Netherlands challenged Iberian dominance. Like the Spanish and Portuguese before them, the English, French, and Dutch hungered for vast riches to plunder in the Americas. Unable to break Spain's domination of Central and South America, they resorted to piracy, illicit trade on the periphery of New Spain, and eventually, colonization of North America. Flush with imperial success and with coffers teeming with bullion, the Spanish undermined their own position by squandering their newfound riches and undertaking ill-fated wars with their northern neighbors. As a result, with the defeat of the Spanish Armada in 1588, power in the Atlantic frontier began to shift toward the Dutch and the English.

The English, French, and Dutch colonies in North America evolved very differently from those of the Spanish. Just as the regimes of England and the Netherlands were far less autocratic than Spain's, so, too, were those of the English and Dutch colonies. For many reasons, New France, New Netherland, and the English colonies engendered a rudimentary type of frontier liberty and emerging economic opportunities without parallel in Europe. The lack of indigenous empires to conquer, better relations with native peoples, the relative weakness of imperial control, and the diversity of the initial settlers all contributed to a greater atmosphere of liberty in the North American settlements. In these new settlements, transplanted Europeans germinated a rough and still indistinct sense of equality.

IDENTIFICATIONS

staple crop agriculture	New France
New Netherland	Giovanni da Verrazzano
Magellan	Martin Luther
Calvinism	Protestant Reformation
northwest passage	Jacques Cartier
Huguenots	Samuel de Champlain
Thirty Years' War	Henry Hudson
Dutch West India Company	Dutch Reformed Church

John Cabot (Giovanni Caboto)

Church of England

Humphrey Gilbert

Spanish Armada

joint-stock company

Jamestown

Pocahontas

Headrights

House of Burgesses

George Calvert

Pilgrims

John Winthrop

Anne Hutchinson

Half-Way Covenant

John Cotton

Stuart Dynasty

Restoration

James Harrington

Society of Friends (Quakers)

Henry VIII, Elizabeth I, Mary I

John Hawkins and Francis Drake

Roanoke Island

London Company

Captain John Smith

Powhatan

royal colony

indentures

proprietary colony

Toleration Act of 1649

Mayflower Compact

covenant theology

Puritanism

Roger Williams

West Indies

Pequot War

Oliver Cromwell

John Locke

Royal African Company

William Penn

CHRONOLOGY

1497	John Cabot reaches North America.
1517	Martin Luther posts Ninety-five Theses on Wittenburg Church, inaugurating the Protestant Reformation.
1524	Giovanni da Verrazzano explores the coast of North America.
1534–1543	Jacques Cartier explores the St. Lawrence Valley.
1558	Accession of Queen Elizabeth I.
1560–1590s	English conquest of Ireland.
1585–1590	Walter Raleigh's three failed attempts to launch a colony off Virginia.
1588	Defeat of the Spanish Armada.
1602	Dutch East India Company chartered.
1603	James I becomes king of England.
1607	Virginia Company founds Jamestown.
1608	Samuel de Champlain founds Quebec.
1609	Henry Hudson sails into Hudson River Valley.
1618–1648	Thirty Years' War.
1619	Virginia House of Burgesses created.
	First African slaves sold in British North America.

1620	Separatists found Plymouth Colony.
1622	Opechancanough attacks Virginia.
1626	Pierre Minuit buys Manhattan Island, establishing New Netherland colony.
1629	Puritans found Massachusetts Bay Colony.
1632	George Calvert founds Maryland.
1636	Harvard College founded.
1636–1638	Roger Williams and Anne Hutchinson found Rhode Island.
1637	New England settlers slaughter Pequot Indians.
1640–1649	First English Civil War.
1641	Massachusetts General Court issues Body of Liberties.
1643	New Netherland carries out the Pavonia Massacre.
1649	Maryland Act of Toleration.
1640s	The sugar revolution and the rise of slavery in Barbados.
1660–1688	Restoration Era.
1660	Charles II becomes king of England.
1660s	Royal African Company established.
1662	Half-Way Covenant.
1663	Louis XIV assumes direct control over New France.
1663–1665	Carolina colony established by Ashley-Cooper.
1664	Duke of York granted charter for New York colony.
1665	New Jersey charter.
1680–1681	William Penn founds Pennsylvania colony.

THEMATIC TOPICS FOR ENRICHMENT

1. Define the various "spiritual frontiers" in the Americas. How important was missionary work in the European settlements?

2. Assess the statement of King Francis I of France that only by occupying a distant land could one acquire a valid claim to it. In what ways was New France a successful colony, and in what ways was it a failure?

3. Describe life in the early Chesapeake Bay area.

4. Discuss the special problems of the New Netherland colony and its attempts to overcome them. How successful were they?

5. Evaluate the Dutch conviction that "frank acceptance of religious diversity might stimulate trade."

6. Compare the demographics of the several New World colonies. Why was the mortality rate in New England so much lower than that in the Chesapeake?

7. What was the Massachusetts 1641 "Body of Liberties," and what precedents did it set?

8. Which was more important in Puritan Massachusetts—toleration or suppression of dissent? Explain.

9. What were the chief differences between class and caste in the American colonies?

10. What was the Puritan Revolution of the 1640s, and what were its effects upon colonial development?

11. Explain the quote: "England discovered its colonies and their importance around 1650."

12. Give a brief overview of the founding of the Restoration Colonies. What do the authors mean by "Far more than New England or Virginia, the Restoration Colonies foreshadowed what the United States became in later centuries"?

13. Which British colonies were proprietorships? Who were the proprietors, and what did they hope to accomplish?

14. Discuss the significance of the Dutch roots of the New York colony.

15. Enumerate and discuss the unique social features of the Pennsylvania colony.

16. What were the causes and the consequences of Bacon's Rebellion in Virginia?

GEOGRAPHY OBJECTIVES

1. Find England, France, and the Netherlands on a map of Europe (p. 16).

2. Draw the triangular route of a Portuguese slave ship from Europe to Africa to Brazil and back to Portugal (p. 41).

3. Identify the following rivers in North America: Saint Lawrence, Charles, Hudson, Delaware, James (p. 60).

4. Find the Leeward Islands, Jamaica, Barbados, and Hispaniola in the Caribbean Sea (p. 67).

5. Compare the sailing routes from Spain and Portugal to the New World with those of England and the Netherlands (p. 16).

6. Compare the extent of British North American settlements before the Restoration with that at the turn of the eighteenth century (p. 92).

SUGGESTED ESSAY TOPICS

1. In what ways did the societies that Europeans created in America differ from one another? In what ways were they similar?

2. Explain the major differences between Catholicism and Protestantism (Calvinism, in particular).

3. How successful were colonists at duplicating the society of their parent cultures?

4. Assess the following statement: "New England proved an ideal model for how to build a colony, while Virginia proved an example of how not to establish one."

5. Explain the development of the Protestant Reformation in Europe, and describe its impact on the development of the American colonies.

SUGGESTED WEB ACTIVITY FOR THE CLASSROOM

Jamestown Rediscovery

   http://www.apva.org/jr.html

This site takes visitors on a virtual tour of the archaeological workings at the restored settlement of Jamestown, Virginia. See past finds, current work, and future plans for the area.

LECTURE OUTLINE

1. The **Protestant Reformation** in Europe provided a **challenge to** the supremacy of **Spain,** and it set the tenor for European conflict based on religious differences.

2. **New France** comprised sparsely settled trading entrepôts primarily along the Saint Lawrence River, where the inhabitants suffered through the frigid winter in order to trade in furs.

   (Show Transparency 2.02: Map, New France and the Jesuit Missions)

   a. **Early French explorers** included Verrazzano and Cartier; they were sent abroad at the behest of King Francis I in an attempt to claim some of the Western Hemisphere for France.

   b. Early **New France** was an underpopulated outpost characterized by missions and the fur trade, but little else.

   c. New France under Louis XIV became better organized and more populous, but the Caribbean proved a greater attraction for many **French immigrants.**

3. The **Dutch and Swedish settlements** of North America in the Hudson River and Delaware Bay areas were primarily trading outposts with little missionary zeal.

   a. Sparsely populated New Netherland was essentially the dominion **of the East and West India Companies,** as the government of the Netherlands had few resources to devote to full-scale colonization of North America.

   b. **New Netherland** became one of the first **pluralistic societies,** by necessity containing ethnic and religious diversity.

   c. **Swedish and English encroachments** on the Dutch led to conflict by the mid-1600s.

4. Increasing numbers of settlers, relative stability, and a growing economy helped to spark a **challenge to all empires from Elizabethan England.**

   a. When the strife of the **English Reformation** finally subsided with the accession of Queen Elizabeth and the permanent establishment of the Anglican Church, England began to look toward the West with new interest.

   b. Before any full-scale colonization, the pirates **John Hawkins and Francis Drake** plundered the Spanish Main in search of gold and glory.

   c. **Sir Humphrey Gilbert,** having brutally colonized **Ireland,** set his sights on establishing settlements in America.

   d. **Sir Walter Raleigh** attempted three successive settlements in the Chesapeake, including Roanoke, but war with Spain preoccupied the queen for some years, hampering early colonization efforts.

5. The seventeenth century marked the **swarming of the English** in successive waves onto the North American shores in numbers unmatched by any other European nation.

   (Show Transparency 2.01: Nova Britannia Brochure promoting Virginia colony; and Transparency 2.04: Map, Virginia Company Charter, 1606)

6. The first permanent English migrations went to **the Chesapeake and the West Indian Colonies,** where their hopes for easy subjugation of local Indians soon were dashed.

   a. The first Chesapeake settlement at **Jamestown** was a **disaster.**
      i. Soon after its founding in 1607, the colony ran out of food and the settlers suffered from devastating illnesses.
      ii. John Smith bullied and cajoled the settlers into taking responsibility for themselves, and they held on until John Rolfe introduced the **colony's salvation—tobacco.**

© 2002 Thomson Learning, Inc.

b. More attention by the Crown led to **reorganization** and **reform,** but continual **crisis** in the first decades of Virginia's history culminated in the replacement of the Virginia Company's charter with royal control.

c. The survival and economic viability of the fledgling colony depended overwhelmingly on **tobacco** and the importation of white **indentured servants.**

d. Charles I granted Lord Baltimore the charter to **Maryland** in 1632. Designed as a haven for Catholics, the colony soon had a majority of Protestants and no truly organized religion.

(Show Transparency 2-05: Map, Virginia and Maryland, circa 1675)

e. A disproportionate number of men, short life expectancies, high rates of illegitimacy, and frequent remarriage among women characterized **Chesapeake family life.**

f. The **West Indies** produced labor-intensive staple crops that virtually guaranteed the **transition to slavery.**

(Show Transparency 2-06: Map, Principal West Indian Colonies in the Seventeenth Century)

g. The **rise of slavery in North America** proved gradual, with few laws distinguishing between white and black until the eighteenth century.

7. Seeking relief from religious persecution, dissenters of all stripes dominated the settlement of the **New England colonies,** but later generations labored to preserve the accomplishments of their ancestors.

(Show Transparency 2-07: Map, New England in the 1640s)

a. The **Pilgrims** fled Europe for Virginia in 1620, but a storm led them to establish the colony farther north than planned.

b. Protestants defined their relationship with God by means of a **covenant theology** articulated by a learned ministry and a devout laity.
   i. Between 1629 and 1639 Puritans established **Massachusetts Bay** with settlers determined to find a "godly home."
   ii. Soon businessmen joined these settlers, threatening their religious stability even while bringing them **economic success.**

c. Close ties of extended families, corporate communities, and church life characterized **Puritan family life** in the seventeenth century.

d. A quest for **conversion,** increasing **dissension,** and territorial **expansion** marked the inevitable movement away from the closed corporate communities of the early years of settlement.

e. Puritans established various forms of self-government through their **congregations, towns, and colony governments.**

f. Controversy over **infant baptism** led to additional **dissent** that caused repeated crises in New England's Congregational churches, the most important of which resulted in the articulation of the **Half-Way Covenant.**

8. The **English Civil Wars** temporarily halted the progress of North American colonization between 1640 and 1660.

9. The **first Restoration Colonies** followed closely on the heels of the restoration of Charles II in 1660, as the king sought to repay his supporters with charters in America.

a. **James Harrington and the aristocratic ideal** of a self-governed land of enlightened landholders figured prominently in the foundation of the Carolinas.

b. The colony of **New York** proved a failed **experiment in absolutism** but thrived as a diverse colony of traders and landowners.

(Show Transparency 2-08: Map, Early Carolina, circa 1710)

10. William Penn founded Pennsylvania as a colony of **brotherly love** dominated by the **Quakers,** whose religious and familial beliefs made the colony unique and attractive for immigrants.

   (Show Transparency 2-10: Map, Early Pennsylvania and New Jersey, circa 1700)

Conclusion: It took the nations of northwest Europe some time to plant colonies in the Western Hemisphere, but by 1600 they had begun to expand in earnest. Within a century, the French, Dutch, and English had effectively challenged Spanish domination of the Atlantic frontier and had firmly established colonies throughout the Atlantic coast of North America. By 1700, England appeared poised to become the overall victor in the quest for colonial empire.

FOCUS ON FEATURES

American Album: The Prince, the Quaker, and the Middle Colonies, p. 76
History Through Film: *Black Robe*, p. 48
Link to the Past: Jamestown Historic Briefs, p. 68

TEACHING RESOURCES

The Magna Carta is an examination of the origins and historical significance of one of the most important documents of Anglo-American political culture. Films for the Humanities (22 minutes).

America: The Newfound Land, narrated by Alistair Cooke, discusses how the British decimated the Indians and out-dueled the Spanish and French for North America. BBC/Time-Life Video (52 minutes).

Colonizing North America: Early Settlements depicts the lives of early settlers, from Jamestown through the turn of the eighteenth century. Filmic Archives (18 minutes).

The Enterprise of England offers an analysis of the reign of Elizabeth I. BBC Video (58 minutes).

America: Home Away from Home examines the Puritan, Pilgrim, and Quaker settlements of the East Coast. Narrated by Alistair Cooke. BBC/Time-Life Video (52 minutes).

Plimoth Plantation reveals the life of Plymouth colony in the year 1627 as told by its "residents." VideoTours History Collection (30 minutes).

Chapter 3

ENGLAND DISCOVERS ITS COLONIES: EMPIRE, LIBERTY, AND EXPANSION

CHAPTER SUMMARY

The seventeenth century witnessed England's simultaneous establishment of far-flung colonies over a thousand miles of British North America and its rise to prominence among its European rivals. Remarkably, these developments occurred during a century of political and social turmoil. By 1700, England could wield great power on both sides of the Atlantic Ocean.

In the aftermath of the Puritan Revolution, Parliament and, later, the restored Stuart monarchy "discovered" England's colonial possessions. The Chesapeake colonies, if not flourishing, had evolved into permanent settlements based largely on tobacco production, while the New England colonies had prospered through commerce. By 1660, Massachusetts itself boasted a population of over forty thousand.

Embracing the principles of mercantilism, the government of Charles II empowered the Lords of Trade to oversee the colonies, in order to ensure the adequate exploitation of the economic potential of those colonial possessions. The centerpiece of the mercantilist doctrine was a set of Navigation Acts whose sole purpose was to make the mother country prosper by regulating trade within the empire. The aim of these Restoration acts was nothing less than to bring order, if not uniformity, to England's far-flung colonial possessions.

The Glorious Revolution of 1688 convulsed the empire on both sides of the Atlantic. The fall of the Stuarts ensured that the power of the monarchy, once it was restored in 1692, would be greatly curtailed. Republican ideals of liberty and checks upon governmental authority took root in the colonies at least as much as, if not more than, in England. After a century of upheaval, warfare, and civil strife, England had become the most powerful nation in Europe, while its citizens—both in England and America—enjoyed substantial liberty.

The Indians suffered greatly from the expansion of provincial America. As European settlers joined their American-born peers in pushing farther inland, they brought with them the same circumstances and behaviors that had so plagued the coastal Indian tribes: diseases, alcohol, and an insatiable desire for land. When the inevitable crisis came, the French and the Spanish proved rather better than the English in working out reasonable solutions. New France won and held the cooperation of most Indians of the interior who lived east of the Mississippi. Although Indians masterfully played off one European power against another, they retreated increasingly farther inland in order to protect themselves and preserve their way of life.

LIBERTY, EQUALITY, POWER: A THEMATIC BRAID

Perhaps in no century was power more "up for grabs" in England than in the seventeenth. Two revolutions and a regicide attest to that. While a monarch ruled the empire at both the beginning and the end of the century, by 1700 his ability to wield arbitrary power had diminished greatly, and the effective power of the English state had inevitably increased. From Oliver Cromwell to John Locke, the English people had explained their successive overthrows of autocratic rulers by appealing to liberty. While only a few radicals agitated for equality, many English subjects fought earnestly for increased personal liberty under the rule of a less-powerful monarchy. In doing so, they developed the basic tenets of republicanism, including constitutionalism, mixed government, and the right of legitimate opposition.

The wild gyrations of revolution and restoration convulsed England's colonies. Every colony witnessed some form of rebellion or unrest, from Bacon's Rebellion in Virginia and Leisler's Rebellion in New York to the Salem witch trials in Massachusetts. By the end of the century, the colonies and the mother country were converging toward representative government in the hope of defending liberty against the encroachment of corrupt central authority. Ultimately, liberty flourished even more in the colonies than it did in the mother country, though more in some colonies than in others.

IDENTIFICATIONS

Mercantilism

enumerated commodities

King Philip's (Metacom's) War

Middle Ground

Dominion of New England

Bacon's Rebellion

Salem witch trials

Imperial federalism

Edmund Andros

Sir Robert Walpole

Louisiana

Popé

Navigation Acts

Lords of Trade

Iroquois Nations

James II

William Berkeley

Glorious Revolution

William III

mixed and balanced Constitution

King William's War

Queen Anne's War

la Salle

Taos Pueblo Revolt

CHRONOLOGY

1651	First of the Navigation Acts.
1675	Metacom's (King Philip's) War begins in New England.
	Lords of Trade created.
1673	Jacques Marquette and Louis Joliet explore the Mississippi.
1676	Bacon's Rebellion in Virginia.
1680	Pueblo Indian Revolt.
1683	New York Charter of Liberties.
1685	James II becomes king of England.
	Louis XIV revokes Edict of Nantes.
1686–1689	Dominion of New England.
1688	Glorious Revolution in England.
1689	Leisler's Rebellion in New York.
	William and Mary ascend to English throne.
	Governor Andros is overthrown in Boston.
	Catholic government is overthrown in Maryland.
1689–1697	King William's War.

1692	Salem witch trials.
1696	Creation of the Board of Trade.
1699	First permanent French settlement in Louisiana.
1702–1713	War of Spanish Succession (Queen Anne's War).
	Act of Union joins England and Scotland.
1714	George I ascends to British throne.
1721–1742	Robert Walpole ministry.

THEMATIC TOPICS FOR ENRICHMENT

1. What were the differences between Whigs and Tories in seventeenth-century England? What contributions did each faction make to the creation of British political culture?

2. How did the Glorious Revolution in England destroy absolutism and guarantee representative government in British North America?

3. In what ways did the Spanish, French, and English empires develop differently from one another?

4. Discuss the ways in which Indian tribes took advantage of—and, in turn, were taken advantage of by—the imperial conflicts among Spain, France, and England.

5. What factors led to a remarkable increase in the population of the British colonies of North America after 1660?

6. In what ways were colonial households similar to their English counterparts, and in what ways were they different?

7. Explain the consequences for both Indians and European settlers of the numerous Indian wars between 1690 and 1716.

GEOGRAPHY OBJECTIVES

1. On a map of Virginia, trace the geographic features of Bacon's Rebellion (p. 106).

2. Identify which British colonies in North America at the beginning of the eighteenth century were royal, proprietary, or corporate (p. 115).

3. Draw the outlines of the North American possessions of Spain and France in the early eighteenth century (p. 120).

4. On a map of North America, fill in the names of the British colonies along the eastern seaboard (p. 115).

SUGGESTED ESSAY TOPICS

1. Discuss the relationship between England's commerce and its colonies.

2. Evaluate the various Indian strategies of survival in North America in the years after European colonization.

3. Define the term *mercantilism* and explain its significance for British colonial policy. In what ways did the Navigation Acts express mercantilistic ideas?

4. What do you think the authors mean by the metaphor "spectrum of settlement" to describe England's colonial possessions (3-2)?

5. Discuss the development of the colonies in terms of demography, race, religion, and economy.

6. Compare and contrast ways of life in the New England, Middle, Chesapeake, and Deep South colonies.

SUGGESTED WEB ACTIVITY FOR THE CLASSROOM

Bacon's Declaration in the Name of the People (30 July 1676)

http://odur.let.rug.nl/~usa/D/1651-1700/bacon_rebel/bacon_i.htm

This site contains the text of Nathaniel Bacon's explanation as to why a rebellion is necessary in Virginia. The text would serve as an effective method for introducing a discussion about John Locke's theory that the people have a right, and even a responsibility, to rebel against an unjust government.

How do Bacon's thoughts seem to suggest the direction colonists will later take with the American Revolution?

LECTURE OUTLINE

1. In many ways the Atlantic Ocean functioned as a prism refracting English aims into **the spectrum of settlement of North America.**

   (Show Transparency 3-2: Map, Area of English Settlement by 1700)

   a. The colonies featured profound demographic differences from one region to the next with New England's invigorating climate at one extreme and the sugar islands of the Caribbean at the other.

   b. The English colonies also featured profound demographic differences among them regarding life expectancy, sex ratios, and family structure.

   c. The colonies also differed along lines of **race** and **ethnicity,** and the types of **economy** they developed.

   d. Significant differences also arose in matters of **religion** and **education,** with colonists in northern regions considering themselves more godly and more literate, the latter of which at least was true.

   e. **Local and provincial government** also varied throughout the colonies, from proprietorships to royal colonies; some colonies boasted rather open, democratic governments, while others proved more autocratic.

   f. The colonies did boast some **unifying trends,** including those of **language, war** (common enemies), **law,** and **inheritance.**

2. The **beginnings of empire** stemmed from England's growing realization that the colonies served vital needs both economically and politically and that the mother country had no coherent colonial policy.

   a. The **critical 1640s** were a time of **upheaval in America,** characterized by Indian warfare, instability, and a general lack of direction from England.

   b. The most important imperial innovation proved to be the **mercantilist** system, which have been called part of a **moral revolution** in which greed replaced glory and love as the primary mover of society.

    c.   Following the Thirty Years' War, Parliament passed the **First Navigation Act,** which banned foreign ships in the colonies, angering independent-minded colonists.

    d.   The **Restoration Navigation Acts** were a crucial series of measures that sought to oversee virtually all aspects of colonial trade, "enumerating" commodities, as well as regulating goods going to and from England's outposts.

3.   As colonists found themselves, both in outlying areas and in their towns, surrounded by Indians, conflicts and conflagrations between **Indians and settlers** became inevitable.

    a.   **Indian strategies of survival** varied greatly, from outright warfare to conversion and alliance.

    b.   Among the most promising, if ultimately unsuccessful, attempts to attain an accommodation between settlers and the local inhabitants were the **Puritan Indian missions,** which sought to bring Indians into the fold of European civilization and thereby end the strife between the two peoples.

    c.   Cultural differences and colonists' insatiable appetite for land led to **Metacom's (or King Philip's) War** in 1675, a bloody conflagration in which some 800 settlers and an unknown number of Indians perished; with the help of their Christian Indian allies, the colonists won the war a year later.

          (Show Transparency 3-03: Map, New England in Metacom's War, 1675–1676)

    d.   **Virginia's Indian War** during the governorship of Sir William Berkeley caused great insecurity on the frontier for several years.

    e.   Led by the recent immigrant Nathaniel Bacon, **Bacon's Rebellion** of 1675–1676 resulted in the devastation of much of Virginia and the temporary collapse of royal government before Bacon died and the rebellion was quashed.

          (Show Transparency 3-04: Map, Bacon's Rebellion in Virginia, 1676)

4.   Bacon's Rebellion helped to trigger a **crisis in England** that led to a **redefinition of empire** in hopes of improving imperial oversight and control.

    a.   The fictional **"Popish Plot," the Exclusion crisis, and the rise of parties** combined to undermine the Catholic Stuart monarchy.

    b.   Indian wars and English politics compelled the Crown to create the **Lords of Trade** and to undertake wholesale **imperial reform** in the colonies in the latter half of the seventeenth century.

    c.   Soon after coming to power in 1685, James II disallowed the New York Charter of Liberties of 1683 and forced New York to join with its northern neighbors to form the **Dominion of New England,** with high-handed Sir Edmund Andros as its governor.

5.   When the birth of a son to James II in 1688 threatened England with a Catholic dynasty, the Parliament invited his Protestant daughter Mary and her husband William to take the throne; during the **Glorious Revolution** the king fled to France.

    a.   Events in England had significant consequences for colonial affairs, leading to what some historians call the **Glorious Revolution in America.**

    b.   The **English response** to the Glorious Revolution in America proved remarkably lenient and sympathetic for the most part, as William and Mary sought reconciliation, not conflict.

    c.   At the time when Massachusetts had virtually no central government, charges of witchcraft convulsed the eastern part of the colony; the **Salem witch trials** resulted in the capital punishment of twenty accused persons and contributed to the demise of Puritan rule.

    d. The Glorious Revolution dispatched absolutism in the colonies and helped to guarantee that the **completion of empire** would put representative government in the colonies on far more sure footing.

        i. **Imperial federalism** is the term used to describe the unprecedented division of power between the center of the British Empire and its American colonies.

       ii. English people on both sides of the Atlantic viewed with pride their unwritten **mixed and balanced Constitution,** which provided for a monarchy tempered by the aristocracy and the common people—a framework designed to limit power and protect liberty.

6. The tenuous coexistence of the **contrasting empires** of England, Spain, and France in America erupted into war after the Glorious Revolution.

    a. The **Taos Pueblo Revolt** of 1680 illustrated the tenuous hold of the Spaniards on the Indians of the southwest and, though eventually quashed, was a harbinger of future problems for Spanish rulers.

    b. Relying more on rationality than force, the colony of **New France** maintained a strong presence in the Great Lakes region in an area called the Middle Ground.

        (Show Transparency 3-06: Map, French Middle Ground, circa 1700)

    c. The two countries were considerably less successful at maintaining peace in their imperial possessions in **French Louisiana and Spanish Texas.**

7. With a population of at least 250,000 settlers by 1700 and an explosive growth rate, the **British colonies** could fairly be called **an empire of settlement.**

    a. The key propellant of **British expansion** was the **colonial household,** the center of economic production and of community life.

    b. Householders carried their quest for independence outside the home, embracing a **voluntaristic ethic** as the personal code of both private and **public life.**

    c. France, Spain, and England devolved into **three warring empires** from **1689 through 1716,** significantly slowing growth in the colonies most involved in the fighting.

(Show Transparency 3-07: Map, Northeastern Theater of War, 1689–1713; and Transparency 3-08: Map, Southeastern Theater of War, 1702–1713)

Conclusion: In the course of the seventeenth century, England became a global giant in large measure on the basis of its American colonies and the important economic role they played in the empire. Fitting perfectly into the mercantilist scheme, colonies served as markets for finished goods and supplied vital raw materials to England. British colonists, cognizant of their importance to the mother country, were confident that their cooperation had made them the freest people on earth.

FOCUS ON FEATURES

American Album: Religious Strife, Liberty, and the Clash of Empires, p. 108
History Through Film: *Three Sovereigns for Sarah*, p. 112
Link to the Past: Witchcraft in Salem Village, p. 114

TEACHING RESOURCES

Where America Began explores the life and culture of seventeenth-century Jamestown. VideoTours History Collection (60 minutes).

Colonial America recalls America's earliest days, when empires were competing for the continent. Mastervision Humanities Series (52 minutes).

Black Robe is a stunning portrait of the challenges facing Jesuit missionaries. Vidmark Films (80 minutes).

Unearthing the Slave Trade shows how archaeologists attempt to reconstruct the lives of African Americans in the colonies. Films for the Humanities (60 minutes).

Indians Among Us describes the upheaval resulting from the clash of cultures between Indians and European settlers. Re-Discovering America (60 minutes).

When the White Man Came describes the distinctive characteristics of some of the major tribes living in North America when Europeans arrived. Films for the Humanities (13 minutes).

Chapter 4

PROVINCIAL AMERICA AND
THE STRUGGLE FOR A CONTINENT

CHAPTER SUMMARY

After 1715, the European colonies in provincial America underwent a transformation from settlement to society. While the colonies of Spain, France, and England developed in quite different ways, each experienced similar strains. Indian problems, inter-colonial warfare, and the great difficulties entailed in moving into the interior of the continent played havoc with even the most farsighted imperial schemes.

Through the first half of the eighteenth century, the three empires in North America fought one another. While the main theater of strife continued to be Europe, the possession of North America became increasingly important. Control of North America promised valuable raw materials, ample space for colonization, and increased control over the Indians. Yet, with so much at stake, neither the Spanish, the French, nor the English had the ability to extinguish the others. Well into the eighteenth century, the English control of North America proved elusive.

Indian problems and imperial strife failed to slow the acceleration of immigration into the colonies. Joined by increasing numbers of Scots and Irish, the English continued to seek a better life in North America. For many, expansion and Anglicization promised greater liberty and an improving standard of living. The British colonies, but not the French or Spanish, also began to participate in the European Enlightenment, partly because they established their own newspapers. In the 1730s and 1740s, the colonists also experienced a massive religious revival—the Great Awakening—the first of its kind in world history.

With the great influx of settlers, England's North American possessions developed characteristics similar to those of the mother country. This process of Anglicization had a profound impact on all aspects of colonial society. Declining dangers on the frontier and a more stable economy benefited many colonists, even while simultaneously exacerbating problems for women, slaves, and the poorest members of society. Anglicization ultimately led to political conflict with England.

By the middle of the eighteenth century, the British empire had achieved imperial domination in North America. After marginal victories in King William's War, Queen Anne's War, and King George's War, Britain and its North American colonies roundly defeated the French in the Seven Years' War, partly because Spain remained neutral for most of that conflict. In no small measure, the year 1763 marked the high point of the empire in both England and North America. It is thus all the more remarkable that relations between the firmly secure colonies and the mother country deteriorated so rapidly after 1763.

While always proclaiming allegiance to king and country, the colonists nevertheless fiercely defended their political rights. Considering themselves equal citizens within the empire, colonists vigorously protected their indigenous political institutions. As in England, colonial politics provided a venue primarily for the well connected. Farmers, laborers, transients, and backcountry folk found themselves on the periphery of the political structure. In the course of the eighteenth century, colonial politics featured a "country" and "court" division similar to that in England. Most disputes erupted between governors and their councils on the one hand, and the colonial assemblies on the other. The former vigorously enforced imperial prerogative, upon which their authority depended, while the latter defended colonial rights and privileges. Through the years of the French and Indian War, colonial governors and assemblies resolved most conflicts amicably, for they needed each other to make the colonies function. As often as not, governors and imperial placemen allowed the colonies to function with a minimum of imperial imposition. In return, placemen made their fortunes and went their way.

The French and Indian War, or the Seven Years' War, abruptly intensified imperial interest in the colonies. While the wars of King William and Queen Anne had spilled over into North America, the French and Indian conflict centered in the colonies. As a result, imperial authority in the form of redcoats, the navy, placemen, and the like, grew steadily in what turned out to be a long and bloody fight. The course of the war and the changes in imperial policy combined to create conflict. Government officials had sworn to prosecute the war most vigorously, but the colonists had grown accustomed to officials who seldom sought to enforce many onerous rules and regulations.

The colonists played their part as members of the empire during the imperial conflicts of the eighteenth century. They well understood that their liberty and freedom, which they so greatly prized, depended on their membership in the British Empire. British power ensured colonial liberty. In time, however, the colonists began to feel that liberty slipping from their grasp.

LIBERTY, EQUALITY, POWER: A THEMATIC BRAID

The expansion and Anglicization of provincial America meant greater liberty and greater power for its inhabitants. By the middle of the eighteenth century, victories over their French and Spanish rivals had afforded colonists a great deal of opportunity and freedom. British power at home fostered colonial liberty.

Expansion and diversification did not begin to bring about true equality. While many colonists enjoyed increased wealth and privileges, they often did so at the expense of others. Some who lost status of one kind or another were opponents of the empire, such as the French, the Spanish, and their Indian allies, while others were part of the empire itself. Expansion into the interior of North America provided opportunity to many, but at significant cost. Indian wars, disease, and brutal living conditions plagued the backcountry, and in every colony, slavery had become an important, often vital, source of labor. Thus, as the availability of slaves increased, colonists' wealth and status became tied to the exploitation of others. By the middle of the eighteenth century, slavery had become one of the mainstays of English liberty, particularly in the southern colonies. Power and liberty had their costs.

Virtually all subjects of the empire agreed that Britain's astonishing rise to great-power status was the result of a unique system of mixed and balanced constitutional government. Imperial victories demonstrated the merits of beneficent government. In sum, British power was essentially intertwined with British liberty.

Similarly, British subjects on both sides of the Atlantic well understood the importance of British imperial vigilance to the maintenance of liberty. The French in Canada and the Spanish in Florida made it particularly clear to colonists that their liberty had a cost. When called upon to make sacrifices for the defense of the empire, the colonists for the most part responded with materiel and manpower, even when not directly threatened. Although they failed to agree to Franklin's Albany Plan, the colonists fought vigorously in the French and Indian War. In the course of nine years of warfare, many colonies played important roles in the final victory. They believed they had defended their liberty with skill and bravery.

IDENTIFICATIONS

gang labor

Charleston

staple crop

redemptioners

Georgia

Benjamin Franklin

James Oglethorpe

Great Awakening

task system

Eliza Lucas Pinckney

Hanoverian dynasty

paper money

John Peter Zenger

Guy Fawkes' Day

Scots-Irish

George Whitefield

Jonathan Edwards

Methodism

de Mosé

Fort Oswego

wampum

War of Jenkins' Ear

Treaty of Aix-la-Chapelle

Albany Congress

French and Indian War

William Pitt

Cherokee War

Baptists

King's College

Fort Louisbourg

Stono Uprising

Louisiana

Fort Duquesne

Acadian expulsion

Ohio Company of Virginia

General Edward Braddock

Fort William Massacre

Peace of Paris

CHRONOLOGY

1704	*Boston Newsletter* becomes first newspaper in British colonies.
1714	George I brings the Hanoverian dynasty to the British throne.
	Yamassee War in South Carolina.
1716	Spanish begin to settle Texas
1722	New Orleans founded.
1727	George II suceeds George I.
1730s–1740s	Great Awakening.
1732–1733	Founding of Georgia.
1733	Molasses Act.
1735	Zenger trial.
1739	George Whitefield's second trip to British colonies.
	Stono Rebellion.
1739–1742	War of Jenkins' Ear.
1741	New York slave conspiracy trials.
1744–1748	King George's War.
1748	Treaty of Aix-la-Chapelle.
1754	Washington surrenders at Great Meadows.
	Albany Congress.
1755	Edward Braddock defeated.
	Acadians expelled.
1756–1763	Seven Years' War (French and Indian War).
1757	William Pitt becomes war minister.
1759	Wolfe defeats Montcalm on Plains of Abraham.
1760	Accession of George III as king of Great Britain.
1760–1761	Cherokee War devastates Carolina backcountry.
1763	Peace of Paris.

THEMATIC TOPICS FOR ENRICHMENT

1. How did the massive influx of African slaves between 1700 and 1740 transform the social structure of the southern colonies?

2. What was "householder autonomy" and what factors threatened to undermine it?

3. How did life in the backcountry differ from that on the coast?

4. Discuss the changing role of women throughout the eighteenth century.

5. Why was the utopian experiment in Georgia such a failure?

6. What were the unique features of South Carolina? Contrast gang labor with the task system.

7. Why were the Mid-Atlantic colonies considered to be the "best poor man's country"?

8. What were the key features of denomination realignment in the Great Awakening?

9. Compare the power of the colonial governors with that of the colonial assemblies.

10. Assess the military aspects of the French and Indian War. In what ways did the conflict lead to misunderstandings between colonists and the mother country?

GEOGRAPHY OBJECTIVES

1. Distinguish the colonies of the Upper South with those of the Lower South (p. 169).

2. Find the Georgia colony on a map. It was meant to be a buffer between which two areas (p. 156)?

3. Locate the main regions where Indian tribes could play off one colonial power against another (p. 159).

4. Find Fort Duquesne, Fort Oswego, and Lake George on a map of North America in the years of the French and Indian War (p. 159).

5. Sketch out the British conquest of Canada from 1758 through 1760. Identify which American colonies were closest to the conflict (p. 168).

SUGGESTED ESSAY TOPICS

1. Discuss the process of Anglicization in the colonies to 1750. How did the colonists seek "to emulate their homeland"?

2. What was the role of religion in the settlement and growth of the North American colonies?

3. Define the term *Enlightenment*. In what ways did colonial development reflect Enlightenment ideas? How widespread were Enlightenment ideas in the colonies?

4. Detail the basic features of government in the American colonies. What were the major similarities and differences between the government of the mother country and that of the colonies?

SUGGESTED WEB ACTIVITY FOR THE CLASSROOM

Project Sugar (Information about the Gullah language and people)

http://www.gcrc.musc.edu/sugar/gullah.html

This site contains descriptions of the Gullah, African Americans from South Carolina and Georgia. Their determination to hold on to their African heritage has brought them some unusual experiences. This site helps students trace their development, both directly and through a link to "Gullah Language and Culture."

LECTURE OUTLINE

1. In the eighteenth century, British colonists tried to reconcile the quickening pace of expansion with England's continued attempts at **Anglicization** of the colonies.

   (Show Transparency 4-01: British Ad [1738] Encouraging Scots-Irish to Move to New York)

   a. As the economy of colonial America became more complex and differentiated, economic inequality led to a **threat to householder autonomy.**

   b. Changes from settlement to a stratified society led colonists toward **Anglicizing the role of women,** by making them more dependent on men and taking away the few rights they had earlier enjoyed in the colonies.

2. The eighteenth century witnessed dramatic changes in North America as territorial expansion and increased immigration brought about **regional differentiation** within the empire.

   a. Immigration and the advent of plantation slavery on a large scale signaled the emergence of the **Old South,** characterized by the production of staple crops for export.

   b. With the phenomenal growth of pluralistic societies in Pennsylvania and New Jersey, the Mid-Atlantic colonies came to be known as the **"best poor man's country."**

   c. Later immigrants such as the Scots-Irish and the Germans found coastal life crowded and moved into the **backcountry,** where they carved out independent, often clannish and violent lives.

   d. In the course of the eighteenth century, New England suffered from a **faltering economy** and currency problems related in part to the circulation of **paper money.**

3. What made these diverse regions of **provincial America** more alike was their slow process of **Anglicization,** or the gradual development of more English characteristics.

   a. Although few colonists owned books or engaged in intellectual debate, the **world of print** was spreading ideas through the colonies, most often through newspapers.

   b. The **Enlightenment in America,** in both its religious and secular forms, transformed colonists' assumptions and modes of thinking.

   c. As in England, **lawyers and doctors** began to emerge as part of a coterie of professionals with growing prestige and power.

   d. Founded in 1732–1733, **Georgia failed as the Enlightenment Utopia** imagined by its founders; it became just another southern colony dominated by slavery and local exigencies.

4. The **Great Awakening** convulsed religious institutions and virtually all of society in provincial America.

   a. The **origins of the revivals** remain obscure but may be tied to the rise of a new generation of ministers with decidedly novel ideas, especially the importance of conversion experiences.

   b. Many historians date the beginning of religious enthusiasm in America to **George Whitefield** launching the **transatlantic revivals,** particularly in his second trip to the colonies in 1739.

   c. The revivals caused **disruptions** in virtually every colony that took years to die down.

   d. Historians have debated the exact **long-term consequences of the revivals,** but they agree that the Great Awakening affected almost every colonial community, often leading to realignments within the various church bodies.

   e. Religious schisms from the revivals resulted in the establishment of a number of **new colleges.**

   f. The **denominational realignment** that ensued from the awakenings is a unique feature of American religion.

5. A mixture of local and English traditions, **political culture in the colonies** developed rapidly in the eighteenth century.

   a. The two key institutional developments were the **rise of the assembly** and the growing responsibilities of **the governor.**

   b. The **southern colonies** had **"Country Constitutions"** that emphasized the importance of restricting corruption and central power.

   c. **"Court Constitutions"** were characteristic of the **northern colonies,** where powerful councils closely advised imperial governors and factions became an important political element.

6. Contention with France and Spain led to a **renewal of imperial conflict** by mid-century.

   a. The colonists, as well as Native Americans there, were eager to offer **challenges to French power** in the interior.

   (Show Transparency 4-02: Map, French Louisiana and Spanish Texas, circa 1730)

   b. The **danger of slave revolts and of war with Spain** grew in the first decades of the century, ultimately culminating in 1739 in the Stono Rebellion and the War of Jenkins' Ear.

   (Show Transparency 4-03: Map, Caribbean Theater of War, 1739–1742)

   c. In 1744, **France** joined Spain to **fight Britain in King George's War,** in which untrained Yankee volunteers subdued the great French fortress of Louisbourg on June 16, 1745.

   (Show Transparency 4-04: Map, Southeastern Theater of War, 1739–1742)

   d. All of these conflicts merely foreshadowed the **impending storm** that would take place after mid-century as colonists continued to pour into new territory.

7. The **war for North America** fought between France and Britain between 1755 and 1763 was popularly known as the French and Indian War.

   (Show Transparency 4-05: Map, France Versus Britain in North America by 1755)

   a. When Britain suggested the colonies convene the **Albany Congress** in 1754, Benjamin Franklin proposed a plan for mutual defense, but the colonies were not yet ready to unite, and Britain determined that such a union would be detrimental in any case.

   (Show Transparency 4-06: Map, British Offensives, 1755)

   b. The first years of the French and Indian War, especially with the death of **General Edward Braddock,** proved to be bitter years filled with **British defeats.**

   c. After Britain declared war on France in 1756, the North American conflict became a **world war** fought throughout Europe as well as in Europe's colonies around the globe.

   d. Years of war and uncertainty led to grave **imperial tensions.** The Earl of **Loudoun** failed to satisfy the Crown's commander of naval forces, but when William **Pitt** became Minister of War in 1757 conditions in the colonial military began to improve.

   (Show Transparency 4-07: Map, Conquest of Canada, 1758–1760)

   e. The years 1758–1760 can be termed the **years of British victory,** as the war finally became clearly winnable.

   (Show Transparency 4.08: Map, Growth of Population to 1760)

   f. In an effort to take advantage of the great burden of England's war with France, southern Indians commenced the **Cherokee War; Spanish intervention** in the war only briefly slowed Britain's march toward victory.

© 2002 Thomson Learning, Inc.

g. The **Peace of Paris** of 1763 changed the face of North America and led colonists and their British counterparts to believe that a new era of peaceful commerce between them was about to begin.

Conclusion: As the colonists of provincial America struggled to secure more land and greater security, they created a socially stratified society of richer and poorer, ins and outs, that during the eighteenth century increasingly came to resemble England. The costs and consequences of a succession of imperial struggles set the stage for the demise of the British Empire in America.

FOCUS ON FEATURES

American Album: The Refined and the Crude, p. 142
History Through Film: *The Last of the Mohicans*, p. 166
Link to the Past: Benjamin Franklin and the Colonial Enlightenment, p. 138

TEACHING RESOURCES

Multicultural Peoples of North America video series. This collection celebrates the varied cultural heritage of different cultural groups. Includes videos on African Americans and the Amish. Filmic Archives (30 minutes each).

Working for the Lord depicts American religious development into the nineteenth century. Republic Pictures Home Video (52 minutes).

The Inventory examines the life of a typical middle-class family in the eighteenth century through an examination of its possessions and values. Films for the Humanities (28 minutes).

Old Salem and *Cavaliers and Craftsmen—Williamsburg* depict life in two of America's oldest communities through both a social and historical approach. VideoTours History Collection (30 minutes each).

Colonial America: Life in the Maturing Colonies focuses on the colonies between the turn of the eighteenth century and the French and Indian War. Filmic Archives (17 minutes).

From Waalstraat to Wall Street explores the development of English New York from its Dutch roots as New Amsterdam. Films for the Humanities (50 minutes).

The Battle of Quebec: 1759, The End of the French and Indian War describes the Battle of Quebec while analyzing the causes of the French and Indian War from a Canadian perspective. Films for the Humanities (32 minutes).

In Search of the Dream: Unearthing the Slave Trade examines slavery in New York City through a close review of the archaeological records unearthed in lower Manhattan. Films for the Humanities (28 minutes).

The Last of the Mohicans is a feature film starring Daniel Day Lewis that gives a strong dramatization of the James Fenimore Cooper tale about the French and Indian War.

Chapter 5

REFORM, RESISTANCE, REVOLUTION

CHAPTER SUMMARY

England's costly victory in the French and Indian War demonstrated the strategic importance of North America to the British Empire. After the signing of the Peace of Paris in 1763, the new Grenville administration wasted little time in implementing a series of measures that demonstrated Britain's commitment to keeping the colonies under greater supervision. The Proclamation Line; the Sugar, Currency, and Quartering Acts; and the fateful Stamp Act put the imperial government on a collision course with the colonies. Colonists of every stripe, from New Hampshire to Georgia, came together as never before in protest against what they perceived to be a great and impossible usurpation of their British rights and liberties.

Through a series of three successive crises, the relationship between Britain and its North American colonies deteriorated to the brink of revolution. When the thirteen colonies declared their independence in 1776, it was not what either side had planned, or even desired, just a decade earlier.

The first imperial crisis stemmed from the Stamp Act of 1765. When Parliament passed the act over the vocal objections of colonists like Benjamin Franklin and a number of members of Parliament, it considered its actions in line with previous imperial measures. The colonists felt differently, believing that the Stamp Act was an attempt to raise revenue, not to regulate trade. As such, it was an unconstitutional attempt by Parliament to confiscate colonists' property; taxation was something only the colonial assemblies could undertake. Through coordinated action and the vigilante activism of the "Sons of Liberty," the colonies (save Georgia) managed to keep stamped paper from ever being circulated. Although Parliament issued a ringing Declaratory Act, it repealed the loathsome and unenforceable Stamp Act. The colonists jubilantly celebrated their victory.

Smarting from the Stamp Act rebuke, many members of Parliament eagerly welcomed Charles Townshend's claim that he had devised a means to impose taxes on the recalcitrant colonists. Townshend argued that the colonies would agree to duties on tea, lead, glass, and other enumerated imports. He would simply couch the duties in terms of the long-standing Navigation Acts. Townshend could not have been more in error. Summarily rejecting his distinction between internal and external taxation, the colonists again organized resistance to parliamentary actions. In this case, they formulated a nonimportation agreement in which colonial merchants would not import British goods. Once again, Parliament eventually backed down, averting a prolonged crisis by repealing all of the Townshend duties except the one on tea.

The third and final crisis stemmed from another fateful act of Parliament—this one designed to induce the colonists to buy duted tea. In response, Boston's Sons of Liberty threw several shiploads of East India Tea Company tea into Boston Harbor. The ensuing severe reaction by Parliament—a group of retaliatory decrees known as the Coercive Acts—precipitated concerted colonial action. The First and Second Continental Congresses took the initial steps toward independence, and by April 1775, the colonists and the British Empire were at war. The actual Declaration of Independence came fifteen months later.

The same misunderstandings, fears, and lack of mutual trust that had led to the imperial crises and the Boston Massacre proved too deep-seated to repair by negotiation. Neither the Olive Branch Petition nor any other attempts at reconciliation could stem the growing movement toward American independence. By July 4, 1776, the colonies had rejected all parliamentary authority and, with the encouragement of Thomas Paine's radical missive, *Common Sense*, they severed their ties to the British monarchy. When the Continental Congress adopted the Declaration of Independence, the United States came into being.

LIBERTY, EQUALITY, POWER: A THEMATIC BRAID

Inevitably, when king and Parliament began a course of imperial reforms in the immediate aftermath of the French and Indian War, the colonists responded with dismay. Convinced they had paid their fair share in defense of their liberty, many colonists argued that the new British attitude toward the colonies now placed that very liberty at risk. This new enemy, if left unchecked, would likewise destroy colonial liberty. Once again, colonists had to defend liberty against overweening power.

In 1776, when Thomas Jefferson declared "all men are created equal," he surely did not mean everyone in colonial America. The colonies on the eve of independence were home to several hundred thousand slaves without the prospect of freedom, as well as a million white women who were legally dependent on men. Jefferson seems to have had in mind a more circumscribed proposition—that colonists and Englishmen ought to enjoy identical political rights. Since king and Parliament proved unwilling to acknowledge colonial rights, the American colonies had to create their own nation.

For the colonies, the movement toward independence was an attempt to protect liberty more than to further it. By 1776, the British Empire, long the protector of colonial liberty, had come to threaten its destruction. The colonies had to take action.

By 1775, only the British army and navy were holding the empire together. Confident of their growing power, which had become apparent in their collective responses to the three successive imperial crises, the American colonies felt compelled to defend their liberty against imperial aggression. The revolutionaries formed the Continental Congress, created a national army, and prepared for a bitter struggle to protect their liberty and demonstrate their equality. They had not yet faced the problem of whether they could protect their liberties without creating a strong central government of their own.

IDENTIFICATIONS

George III

Proclamation of 1763

Pontiac's War

Quartering Act

Sons of Liberty

Stamp Act Congress

Patrick Henry

William Pitt

regulator movement

feudal revival

Gaspée affair

Phillis Wheatley

Thomas Hutchinson

Thomas Gage

Quebec Act

Continental Congress

Olive Branch Petition

Thomas Paine

Declaration of Independence

Paul Revere

Grenville Administration

Paxton Boys

Sugar Act

Stamp Act

virtual representation

nonimportation agreements

Massachusetts Circular Letter

Letters of a Pennsylvania Farmer

Battle of Alamance Creek

Boston Massacre

Tea Act

Revenue Act of 1766

Townshend Revenue Act

Coercive Acts (Intolerable Acts)

Battle of Bunker (Breed's) Hill

Battles of Lexington and Concord

Committee of Public Safety

Common Sense

CHRONOLOGY

1763	Peace of Paris.
	George Grenville administration begins.
	Pontiac's War.
	Proclamation of 1763.
1764	Sugar and Currency Acts passed by Parliament.
1765	Stamp and Quartering Acts passed.
	Rockingham replaces Grenville.
1765–1766	First Imperial Crisis.
1766	Pitt replaces Rockingham.
	Revenue Act passed.
1767	Townshend Duties passed by Parliament.
	Grafton replaces Pitt.
	John Dickinson publishes *Letters*.
1767–1770	Second Imperial Crisis.
1768	John Hancock's sloop *Liberty* seized.
1770	Boston Massacre.
1771	Regulators defeated at Alamance Creek, North Carolina.
1772	British customs vessel *Gaspée* burned.
	Colonies create committees of correspondence.
1773	Tea Act passed by Parliament.
	Boston Tea Party.
1773–1776	Third Imperial Crisis.
1774	Quebec Act.
	Coercive Acts imposed.
	First Continental Congress.
1775	Battles of Lexington and Concord.
	Second Continental Congress.
	Battle of Bunker Hill.
	Lord Dunmore's Proclamation.
	Olive Branch Petition sent to King George III.
1776	Thomas Paine publishes *Common Sense*.
	Battle of Dorchester Heights.
	Battle of Moore's Creek Bridge.
	Declaration of Independence.

THEMATIC TOPICS FOR ENRICHMENT

1. How did Britain define "virtual representation"? Explain why the colonies so vigorously rejected the idea. Why did they similarly decline actual representation in Parliament?

2. Why did Parliament repeal the Stamp Act? What was the point of repealing the Stamp Act, yet passing the Declaratory Act?

3. How legitimate was the colonial distinction between regulation and taxation? Was there any precedent for such a distinction in English history? Explain.

4. What was the "feudal revival"? Assess its significance for Revolutionary America.

5. Discuss the meaning of liberty to women and slaves. How was it distinct from the liberty of white males?

6. How did the government of George III change its tactics for punishing the colonies after the Boston Massacre, the *Gaspée* affair, and the Boston Tea Party? How accurate is the statement that by the third imperial crisis, the empire held together solely by force?

GEOGRAPHY OBJECTIVES

1. Trace the extent of the Proclamation Line of 1763 (p. 177).

2. Locate the colonies in which the great estates of the feudal revival covered the largest extent of land (p. 194).

3. Find Lexington and Concord in relation to the city of Boston (p. 205).

SUGGESTED ESSAY TOPICS

1. The historian Lawrence Henry Gipson once argued that, if there had been no French and Indian War, the American Revolution would not have occurred, at least not when it did. Make a case both for and against Gipson's claim.

2. Some historians have claimed that the era of the American Revolution was characterized by paranoia. Does this description make sense? What underlying fears drove Britain into its imperial reforms? What aspects of these reforms made the colonies fear for their liberties? Were these fears justified on either side? On both sides?

3. How did thirteen disparate colonies that had failed all attempts at collective actions before 1763 manage to unite and declare their independence by 1776?

4. Which actions by the British Parliament appear to have upset the American colonists most during the 1760s and 1770s? Why do you think those specific elements caused more trouble than others?

SUGGESTED WEB ACTIVITY FOR THE CLASSROOM

Virtual Tour of Betsy Ross' Home

www.ushistory.org/betsy/index.html

This site provides a brief history of the house. It includes fifty photos in a pictorial virtual tour. Students can click on the tour from this home page.

LECTURE OUTLINE

1. King and Parliament began a large-scale process of **imperial reform** in response to waging a costly war in North America.

a. The **Bute ministry,** led by the King's principal advisor, John Stuart, began the first steps toward reducing Britain's foreign financial obligations.

b. The subsequent **Grenville ministry** inaugurated an ambitious program intended to effect greater control over the colonies, augmenting revenues in particular.

c. Tailored to meet treaty obligations, **Grenville's Indian policy** rested on the **Proclamation Line of 1763,** which sought to restrict colonists' encroachment onto Indian lands; but Grenville's policy and even **Pontiac's War** failed to halt—or even slow down—European penetration into the continent's interior.

(Show Transparency 5-02: Map, Pontiac's War and the Proclamation Line of 1763)

d. The **Sugar Act** sought to increase revenue and inhibit smuggling by simultaneously lowering duties on molasses and making it more profitable for customs officers to prosecute violators of the Navigation Acts than to take bribes from them.

e. Following closely on the heels of the Sugar Act, the **Currency Act and the Quartering Act** respectively constituted bold new regulation of colonial "paper" currency and restated the colonists' obligations to quarter his majesty's troops.

f. The **Stamp Act** sought to raise revenue in the colonies by taxing all official documents as well as newspapers, pamphlets, and playing cards.

2. Colonial dismay at the Stamp Act and the other parliamentary initiatives since 1763 climaxed in the **Stamp Act Crisis,** as colonists gathered in a Stamp Act Congress to fight Parliament.

a. By means of the nonimportation agreement of the Stamp Act Congress and the extralegal initiatives of the **Sons of Liberty,** the colonies sought **nullification** of the Stamp Act.

b. Colonial vigilance and pressure from London's suffering merchant community forced Parliament to **repeal** the dreaded stamp tax, while simultaneously passing the **Declaratory Act** and the Revenue Act of 1766.

3. Relative quiet returned to imperial relations until the eruption of the **Townshend crisis** in 1767.

a. Named for the Chancellor of the Exchequer, the **Townshend program** was an ill-fated attempt to raise revenue through "external" taxation on colonial imports such as lead, china, and tea.

b. As **resistance** to external taxation grew, Massachusetts once again led the politics of escalation, calling for more widespread **nonimportation** agreements.

c. Parliament's 1768 **experiment in military coercion** accomplished little more than to convince many colonists that the British government was openly seeking to undermine their liberty.

d. As colonials saw parallels between their situation and that of John Wilkes, the **second Wilkes crisis** in England reinforced colonial convictions that the King and Parliament were corrupt, power hungry, and determined to destroy colonial liberties.

e. The **Boston Massacre** of March 5, 1770, marked the failure of Britain's first attempts at military coercion and served to galvanize anti-imperial sentiment throughout North America.

(Show Transparency 5-01: "The Bloody Massacre" woodcut by Paul Revere)

f. **Despite the repeal** of the Townshend taxes and several of the more onerous acts, **disaffection** set in between colonists and mother country.

4. After the second imperial crisis, the **contagion of liberty** caused the colonists to face many **internal cleavages** over their diverging attitudes toward Britain.

a. Although the colonies were moving away from British political domination, many regions, from New York to the Carolinas, witnessed what historians call a **feudal revival,** with the great landlords fanning rural discontent among displaced farmers.

© 2002 Thomson Learning, Inc.

b. The **regulator movements in the Carolinas** resulted from the remarkable under-representation of rural folk in the low-country dominated houses of assembly and left North Carolina bitterly divided over loyalty to Britain.

c. From the growing antislavery movement in the colonies to wives offering their willing support to nonimportation, **slaves and women** responded in a number of meaningful ways to colonial discussions of freedom and liberty.

5. The **last imperial crisis** broke the relative calm of the period 1770–1773, as colonists and mother country failed to resolve amicably their simmering differences.

a. The **tea crisis** resulted in the Boston Tea Party of December 16, 1773, when angry Bostonians threw East India Company tea into Boston Harbor to protest British manipulation of their economy.

b. Britain's response to the Tea Party was a set of **Coercive Acts** which, among other things, shut down Boston's port and revoked the Massachusetts charter, with the intent to force colonial submission.

c. Instead of restoring order, the Intolerable Acts, as the colonists styled them, resulted in a **radical explosion,** which cowed those who had cautioned against rash actions against England.

d. Acting as the voice of the united colonies, the **First Continental Congress** met in Philadelphia in September 1774 and petitioned the king for no new legislation without consent.

e. England's intransigence and colonial unity precipitated the Battles of Lexington and Concord, which inevitably moved the empire **toward war.**

   (Show Transparency 5-03: Map, Lexington, Concord, and Boston, 1775–1776)

6. From the spring of 1775 into the next year, the colonists and Britain fought an **improvised war** in and around Massachusetts, with neither side yet prepared for an all-out conflict.

a. The **Second Continental Congress,** which met in Philadelphia in May 1775, organized national defense and acted as the executive for the continent, since the colonists could no longer trust Parliament with that role.

b. The colonists' **war against Britain** gained **legitimacy** from 1775 to 1776, with the British suffering numerous defeats that caused them to withdraw temporarily from the continent.

c. **Independence** came with the signing of the Declaration of Independence in July 1776, just as Britain landed a large armada of reinforcements and prepared for a fierce fight.

Conclusion: In the aftermath of the Peace of Paris of 1763, three successive imperial crises convinced England that the colonies desired nothing short of independence, and the colonists that king and Parliament sought to destroy their liberties through an overarching imperial power. The result of these almost paranoid views was the disintegration of the empire and the onset of war.

FOCUS ON FEATURES

American Album: American Artists and the Revolution in Painting, p. 200
History Through Film: *1776*, p. 210
Link to the Past: "'The Decisive Day Is Come': The Battle of Bunker Hill," p. 206

TEACHING RESOURCES

Liberty: The American Revolution, volumes I–III, tells the story of the coming of the American War for Independence by means of actors reading contemporary writings. PBS Video (60 minutes each).

Private Yankee Doodle views the life and suffering of the average American soldier in the Revolutionary War through the re-creation of a Continental Army encampment. Films for the Humanities (28 minutes).

To Keep Our Liberty: Minutemen of the American Revolution traces the growing movement toward independence through the eyes of one American patriot. National Park Service Video (35 minutes).

Meet George Washington is a humanizing portrait of Washington as a Virginia planter and colonial businessman who reluctantly assumes a leadership role in the politics of a new nation. Filmic Archives (60 minutes).

Samuel Adams portrays the life and significance of the man who helped create the Sons of Liberty, led the Boston Tea Party, and served in the Continental Congress. Filmic Archives (10 minutes).

Independence, as directed by John Huston, details the dramatic events that led to America's Declaration of Independence in 1776. MPI Home Video (30 minutes).

America: Making a Revolution details the blunders of the imperial government, the increasing colonial agitation for reform, and, ultimately, independence. BBC/Time-Life Video (52 minutes).

1776 is a rollicking musical based on the Broadway hit that celebrates the founding of the United States. Facets Multimedia (approx. 120 minutes).

Chapter 6

THE REVOLUTIONARY REPUBLIC

CHAPTER SUMMARY

Declaring independence on July 4, 1776, proved to be only the beginning of a great struggle for the American people. In the course of the next decade, they defeated the vaunted British army in a prolonged conflagration, fought loyalists in a civil war, wrote constitutions in each new state, and, finally, in 1787 composed the Constitution of the United States.

The Revolutionary War was far longer and more costly than either the Americans or the British could have predicted in 1776. When given a choice, most Indians and most slaves sided with the British. Fighting against the strongest navy in the world and one of Europe's best armies, the American state militias and the Continental Army led by George Washington demonstrated exceptional enthusiasm at the beginning of the war. After numerous setbacks during the course of 1776, including the loss of New York City and most of New Jersey, America's "Spirit of '76" began to wane. Only Washington's daring victories at Trenton and Princeton in December 1776 and January 1777 salvaged the campaign and rekindled America's patriotic fervor.

The Revolutionary War dragged on for five more years. In spite of many grave problems, including a hopelessly weak Congress, an ill-prepared, ill-fed, and almost unpaid army and more defeats than victories, American soldiers and civilians persevered. Encouraged by triumphs at Bennington and especially Saratoga in 1777, the French government formed an alliance with the United States at the beginning of 1778. Within the year, the Spanish had declared war on the British Empire as well. Finally, on October 19, 1781, Washington's army forced the surrender of Lord Cornwallis's army of eight thousand men at Yorktown, Virginia, and Lord North's government resigned in early 1782. Within a year, the British recognized American independence by signing the Treaty of Paris. The Revolutionary War was over.

While soldiers were fighting the war, civilians and politicians were constructing new governments in each state. Without the legitimating force of the monarchy, they fell back on the theory of "popular sovereignty." The people themselves, at first through their legislatures, but eventually through constitutional conventions, created the means by which they would govern themselves. The Articles of Confederation, drafted in 1776 and 1777, proved rather ineffectual. Hamstrung by great deficiencies, particularly lack of the power to tax, the Congress proved far too weak; but it did pass the Northwest Ordinance of 1787, which provided for new states to be admitted to the Union as full equals of the original thirteen. When the Constitutional Convention met in Philadelphia in the summer of 1787, the members decided to scrap the Articles entirely. In the ensuing four months, they constructed an entirely new government with vastly increased powers and a system of checks and balances. By creating separate and independent branches of government, establishing a bicameral legislature, and staggering elections, the Constitutional Convention created a remarkably resilient balance of liberty and power.

LIBERTY, EQUALITY, POWER: A THEMATIC BRAID

The Revolutionary War taught Americans a great deal. While not everyone learned the same lessons, few came away from the experience without a great respect for power on the one hand, and a healthy fear of it on the other. That the American people defeated a far stronger British army proved the power of a republican citizenry. Americans had demonstrated their ability to defend liberty. The new challenge was to ensure that no Americans would usurp anyone else's hard-fought liberty. In a nation dedicated to the ideal that "all men are created equal," yet beset by inequality, a new form of government had to be devised. Based on "popular sovereignty," it had to be powerful enough to preserve liberty, while at the same time protecting the weak from the powerful. By 1804, slaves won at least gradual liberation in every northern state.

The solution, the United States Constitution, satisfied no one completely. Its composers called it a "great compromise" between big states and small states, slave-holding and free states, East and West, and claimed that it accommodated both central and local power. Some thought it a great mistake, giving far too much power to a central government that would prove to be beyond the reach of all but the most powerful citizens. For most Americans, however, the grave weaknesses of the Articles of Confederation convinced them that only greater central power could ensure American liberty. When New Hampshire ratified the Constitution in June 1788, Americans had created a new government with what promised to be a balance of liberty, equality, and power.

IDENTIFICATIONS

Republicanism
Articles of Confederation
Benedict Arnold
Nathanael Greene
Battle of Princeton
John Burgoyne
Brandywine Creek
Marquis de Lafayette
Vergennes
Thoughts on Government
Bicameralism
Loyalists
Battle of Cowpens
Yorktown
Daniel Boone
Three-fifths compromise
New Jersey, Virginia Plans
"necessary and proper" clause
Massachusetts Constitution
Jay Treaty

Lord North
Northwest Ordinance
Battle of Trenton
Lord Cornwallis
The Howes
Continental Army
Valley Forge
Battle of Saratoga
popular sovereignty
separation of powers
Constitutional Convention
Joseph Brant
Robert Morris
Treaty of Paris
Wilderness Road
Daniel Shays
The Federalist
Pennsylvania Constitution of 1776
Annapolis Convention

CHRONOLOGY

1775	Daniel Boone leads first settlers to Kentucky.
1776	Virginia Constitution and Bill of Rights.
	Declaration of Independence.
	Battles of Long Island and Trenton.
1777	Battles of Princeton, Bennington, and Bemis Heights.
	The Howes take Philadelphia, and Congress flees.
	Burgoyne surrenders at Saratoga.

1778	Franco–American treaties signed.
	Battle of Monmouth Court House.
1778–1781	British offensive in the South.
1780	Massachusetts Constitution.
	Benedict Arnold's treason.
1781	Maryland ratifies the Articles of Confederation.
	Lord Cornwallis surrenders at Yorktown, Virginia.
1782	Resignation of Lord North as prime minister.
1783	Treaty of Paris.
1786	Virginia enacts Jefferson's Statute for Religious Freedom.
	Shays's Rebellion in western Massachusetts.
1787	Constitutional Convention meets in Philadelphia.

THEMATIC TOPICS FOR ENRICHMENT

1. Assess the authors' statement that the Revolution "was a civil war in its own right" (see p. 206).

2. Define the terms *republicanism* and *popular sovereignty*. How were they manifested in the era of the American Revolution?

3. Why did Americans begin to think increasingly in terms of race in the era of the American Revolution? What was the "first emancipation"?

4. Explain the weaknesses of the Articles of Confederation. Why did the Second Continental Congress create such a weak body?

5. What mistakes did the British make in their attempt to win over the hearts and minds of the Americans during the early stages of the war?

6. Discuss the similarities and differences between some of the state constitutions written during the Revolutionary War. In what ways did Massachusetts redefine constitutionalism?

7. Who was likely to be a loyalist and who to be a patriot in the American Revolution? How frequently did people change sides during the war?

8. How did the Continental Congress finance the war?

9. What were the main differences between a "cosmopolitan" and a "localist"?

GEOGRAPHY OBJECTIVES

1. Trace the march of the British troops from New York City to Philadelphia. In what state were by far the most battles of the first three years of the Revolutionary War fought (p. 216)?

2. Trace General Howe and General Burgoyne's planned march from the South and North, respectively. Which states would have been cut off from the rest (p. 216)?

3. Locate the major battles of the war in the Lower South in 1780 and 1781 (p. 231).

4. Explain the tactical error Cornwallis made by stationing his army at Yorktown (p. 239).

5. Which states had western land claims at the time of the Revolution (p. 246)?

SUGGESTED ESSAY TOPICS

1. On what basis did Americans reconstruct authority during the American Revolution? What replaced the power and authority of the monarchy? What new institutions were devised to secure authority?

2. Contrast the Articles of Confederation and the Constitution in terms of liberty and power. Was the Constitution a fulfillment of the Revolution or a reaction to its excesses?

3. In what ways did the movement toward independence transform American life? Be sure to discuss politics, economics, and social issues in your answer.

4. After the middle of the eighteenth century, what options did Indians still have in responding to the encroachment of settlers? How had Indian behavior changed since the Iroquois mourning wars of the seventeenth century?

5. Discuss the problems with the Articles of Confederation that led to the Constitutional Convention. How did the government operate under the Articles? In what ways were they not workable?

6. Describe the development of the Constitution at the Constitutional Convention. What were the major problems that had to be solved? What agreements did the representatives reach?

SUGGESTED WEB ACTIVITY FOR THE CLASSROOM

George Washington's Mount Vernon Estate & Gardens

   www.mountvernon.org

This extensive site includes lengthy virtual tours of the mansion and the grounds. Many other interesting items are located here as well.

LECTURE OUTLINE

1. The Revolutionary War was as much a struggle for **hearts and minds** as it was one of competing armies, as the conflict turned on social issues as well as political ones, especially early on in the **northern war of 1776–1777.**

    a. The **British offensive** of 1776 succeeded in gaining ground and wreaking havoc in New York and New Jersey, but hopes of convincing their opponents to capitulate kept British military commanders from completely annihilating their foes.

       (Show Transparency 6-02: Map, Revolutionary War in the Northern States)

    b. The **Trenton–Princeton campaign** proved to be crucial successes for Washington's army, predominantly insofar as it helped keep alive the "Spirit of '76."

2. The **campaigns of 1777 and foreign intervention,** particularly of the French after Saratoga, proved to be the turning points of the war.

    a. Despite the **loss of Philadelphia,** the Continental Army continued to fight, even when it could not defend the nominal capital of the nation and as the Continental Congress virtually disbanded.

    b. John Burgoyne's army of 7,800 surrendered to American forces under the command of Horatio Gates at **Saratoga** on October 17, 1777.

    c. **French intervention and recognition,** which proved critical to ultimate triumph, came almost immediately after the signal victory at Saratoga.

    d. **Spanish expansion and intervention,** also in the aftermath of Saratoga, greatly assisted the American war efforts, particularly insofar as the Spanish forced the British to spread their forces even more thinly.

3. With the Declaration of Independence and the withdrawal of many Tories, Americans faced the uncertain challenge of the **reconstitution of authority.**

    a. In his pamphlet *Thoughts on Government*, **John Adams** proposed a separation of powers as a way to redistribute America's governmental authority.

    b. The **Virginia Constitution,** which contained a declaration of rights drafted by George Mason, served as a model for other states to follow.

(Show Transparency 6-01: Cartoon, The Federal Edifice, celebrating New York's Ratification of the New Constitution)

    c. More radical than that of Virginia, the **Pennsylvania Constitution** and its unicameral legislature and plural executive never really worked as its framers had envisioned.

    d. John Adams and his colleagues in **Massachusetts redefined constitutionalism,** incorporating a unique system of checks and balances, and submitting its drafted constitution to town meetings for ratification.

    e. A lack of power and a deep distrust of central authority plagued the **Confederation** of the states throughout the revolutionary period, causing the Continental Congress to lose most of its power to the new state governments.

4. The **crisis of the Revolution** in the years 1779–1783 resulted from the fact that the war dragged on at great social and personal cost for more than six years.

    a. The **loyalists** were many in number and often struggled with the fact that they supported ideas of British liberty while simultaneously opposing the war.

    b. The lot of **loyalist refugees, black and white,** proved harsh, as many thousands emigrated under duress to Canada and other British territories.

    c. The **Indian struggle for unity and survival** during the war ran the gamut from opposition to England, to awesome frontier violence against American troops.

(Show Transparency 6-03: Map, War on the Frontier, 1777–1782)

    d. After 1778 the war became one of **attrition,** with the **British** plagued by doubts about their ability to win and the Americans plagued by **economic woes.**

5. Perhaps the most gruesome events of the Revolutionary War took place during the **British offensive in the South,** which included Clinton's virtual destruction of Charleston, South Carolina.

(Show Transparency 6-04: Map, War in the Lower South, 1780–1781)

    a. The **partisan war** often pitted native-born Tories against patriots in vicious confrontations which the patriots came to win more and more frequently.

    b. The British offensive and the partisan warfare that ensued led to **mutiny and reform** in the ranks of the Continental army as well as in the militias, and to not very successful efforts at reform in the Congress.

    c. The final stages of the war in 1781 included Cornwallis's **ravaging of Virginia,** his surrender at **Yorktown** in October, and subsequent peace negotiations.

(Show Transparency 6-05: Map, Virginia and the Yorktown Campaign)

6. Years warfare and independence from Britain inevitably led to a **revolutionary society** that few had imagined a decade earlier.

   a. Several of the most profound changes in society were the **religious transformations,** which included increasing religious toleration and the growth of denominationalism.

   b. The fervor of revolutionary sentiment convinced virtually all the North, and much of the upper South as well, to manumit its slaves in what historians call the **first emancipation.**

   c. Revolutionary ideology constituted a **challenge to patriarchy** at the war's end, with women who had wholeheartedly participated in the war effort seeking and sometimes achieving greater legal recognition.

   d. Simultaneous with the defeat of the British was a renewed thrust **of western expansion and conflict with Indians** that would take several decades to resolve.

   e. One of Congress's last acts was the passage of the **Northwest Ordinance,** which would ultimately bring several new states into the Union on equal footing with the original thirteen.

(Show Transparency 6-06: Map, Western Land Claims during the Revolution; and Transparency 6-07: Map, Advance Settlement to 1790)

7. After of the strains and trials of the decade of revolution, many Americans called for the wholesale revision of the Articles of Confederation and the creation of a **more perfect union.**

   a. No one precipitating factor led to the Constitutional Convention; rather, a combination of problems with **commerce, debt,** currency, and **Shays's Rebellion** contributed to the growing discontent with the Articles.

   b. Sectionalism began to emerge almost immediately, as the struggle over the government of the Union became one of **cosmopolitans versus localists.**

   c. During the summer of 1787, participants at the **Philadelphia Convention** drafted the Constitution, scrapping the Articles altogether.

   d. After a tremendous struggle for **ratification,** the new Constitution was confirmed when New Hampshire, the ninth state, voted to accept it.

Conclusion: Despite daunting odds and the dangers of what amounted to a civil war, the Americans managed to persevere through years of warfare, economic tribulations, and weak leadership to defeat the British. Imperial ineptitude greatly enhanced the Americans' chances for victory. That victory was accompanied by significant social upheaval that caused grave problems under the Articles of Confederation, leading in just a few years to the development of a new, stronger Constitution.

FOCUS ON FEATURES

American Album: Toward Equality: The Affectionate Family, p. 244
History Through Film: *The Patriot,* p. 234
Link to the Past: Spy Letters of the American Revolution: The Infamous Benedict Arnold, p. 236

TEACHING RESOURCES

Abigail Adams discusses the life of this important American in light of the changing attitudes toward women in the era of the American Revolution. Filmic Archives (30 minutes).

Liberty: The American Revolution, volumes IV–VI, offers a broad, well-narrated portrait of the Revolutionary War, with particular emphasis on the military campaigns. PBS Video (55 minutes each).

The Battle of Yorktown: 1781 examines the origins of the Revolution, culminating in the British surrender at Yorktown, from a long-term perspective. Films for the Humanities (30 minutes).

Christmas 1783 celebrates America's victory over the British from the perspective of Annapolis, Maryland, where George Washington went to resign as commander in chief before the Confederation Congress. Films for the Humanities (28 minutes).

Fighting for Independence: The Revolutionary War reenacts the major events of the war, political and military, from a number of perspectives. Filmic Archives (20 minutes).

George Mason and the Bill of Rights focuses on the Virginia Ratifying Convention and the debates over the federal Constitution. ETV Video through Social Studies School Service (50 minutes).

Breaking Colonial Ties: Declaration of Independence explains the patriot and Tory viewpoints in Revolutionary America and examines the position of women, slaves, and Native Americans in the debate. Filmic Archives (20 minutes).

Valley Forge: The Battle for Survival uses dramatic reenactments to illustrate daily life in Washington's army during the terrible winter of 1777–1778, as the military commander worked to turn his ragtag men into an army. Films for the Humanities (22 minutes).

Chapter 7

THE DEMOCRATIC REPUBLIC, 1790–1820

CHAPTER SUMMARY

The period from 1790 to 1820 brought geographical expansion and economic diversification to America. The growth of the new nation affected all Americans, as politics and culture changed dramatically. From New England seaports and southern plantations to the Appalachian frontier, America was becoming a democratic republic. Some benefited greatly from these changes, but many did not.

Farmers, artisans, and yeomen, who for so long had felt comfortable with a rough "agrarian republicanism," discovered they were living in a world that was undergoing rapid transformation. Most farmers found themselves increasingly insecure, often maintaining their economic status by having wives and daughters perform outwork of one sort or another. Providing for their children's future became all but impossible. Sons moved away when they could, while daughters were forced to marry much later in life. The growth of overseas trade and the concomitant rise of seaboard towns provided some opportunity for economic independence. Ultimately, achieving a simple "competence" gave way to searching for markets and striving for money.

Society and economy in southern states changed significantly at the turn of the nineteenth century. Chesapeake farmers moved away from slave labor as they produced foodstuffs, while planters in the rapidly expanding Deep South undertook large-scale production of cotton. The growing English demand for raw cotton and Eli Whitney's invention of the cotton gin suddenly made cotton planting hugely profitable. Like many of his fellow Virginians, Thomas Jefferson, who penned the Declaration's "all men are created equal," sold his slaves southward instead of freeing them. While the free black population grew rapidly in the aftermath of the Revolution, the slave population ballooned in much of South Carolina, Georgia, and the new states of the Southwest. Even the admonition of Methodist minister John Wesley that slavery was a great injustice in the eyes of God failed to slow America's recommitment to slavery.

Nowhere was the growth of the democratic republic more obvious than in the backcountry. Settlers poured through the Cumberland Gap and traversed the National Road into the West. Kentucky and Tennessee followed Vermont as the fifteenth and sixteenth states, while Ohio and Louisiana joined the Union shortly thereafter. With the admission of Maine and Missouri in 1820–1821, America boasted twenty-four states.

LIBERTY, EQUALITY, POWER: A THEMATIC BRAID

The Jeffersonian vision of an America of self-sufficient farmers and artisans never really existed, yet the ideal of "agrarian republicanism" continued to appeal to many Americans in the years after the Revolution. Jeffersonians stressed the grave dangers inherent in all forms of power, believing that the sole adequate means to protect liberty rested with virtuous farmers, artisans, and yeomen, whose freedom and independence enabled them to be good citizens and patriots.

Republicans like Thomas Jefferson vigorously defended equality, particularly in the face of those who stressed the interests of the elite. Republicans at the same time restricted equality, denying rights to many Americans, including free blacks and women. Since independence was essential to gaining equality, only those who owned their own property could be trusted with republican liberty.

While Jeffersonians controlled much of the national government in the decades after independence, they could do very little to secure their vision of America. As president, Jefferson managed to curtail the size of the government and virtually double the size of the nation, but his successors did not fare as well. The War of 1812 and the tremendous growth of the economy forced the Republicans to abandon their plans for a nation of farmers. Most Americans gradually began to produce for market, simultaneously making themselves more prosperous and less secure.

IDENTIFICATIONS

H. St. John de Crevecoeur

Notes on the State of Virginia

barter/cash

Cumberland Gap

Fallen Timbers

Old Northwest

William Henry Harrison

Tecumseh

Eli Whitney

freehold

Alexis de Tocqueville

Cane Ridge

Gabriel's Rebellion

competence

outwork

agrarian republicanism

Five Civilized Tribes

Treaty of Greenville

Prophetstown

Tenskwatawa

Battle of Tippecanoe

John Jacob Astor

deism

camp-meeting revivals

John Wesley

Saint Domingue

CHRONOLOGY

1782	Crevecoeur publishes his *Letters of an American Farmer*.
1789	National government commences under the Constitution.
1791	Vermont becomes the fourteenth state.
1792	Kentucky becomes the fifteenth state.
1793	Eli Whitney invents the cotton gin.
	Anglo–French War begins.
1794	Anthony Wayne's Third Army is victorious at Fallen Timbers.
1795	Treaty of Greenville signed.
1796	Tennessee becomes the sixteenth state.
1799	Successful slave revolution in Saint Domingue.
1800	Gabriel's Rebellion in Virginia.
1801	First camp meeting at Cane Ridge, Kentucky.
1803	Jefferson purchases Louisiana Territory from France.
	Ohio becomes the seventeenth state of the Union.
1811	Battle of Tippecanoe.
1812	War of 1812 commences.

© 2002 Thomson Learning, Inc.

THEMATIC TOPICS FOR ENRICHMENT

1. Define the term *competence*. Explain how the goal of competence was distinct from the more contemporary goal of "getting rich."

2. What were the basic beliefs of "agrarian republicanism"? Why was the ownership of property so important in the republican theory?

3. How did the rise of markets change the lives of various Americans from farmers and artisans to frontiersmen and slaves?

4. What were the major factors in the destruction of the Woodlands Indians? Why did "many Indian societies sink into despair"?

5. What was meant by the epithet "our white savages"? Who might call a frontiersman by such a name?

6. In what ways did slaves' lives change in the years after American independence?

7. Why might the first decades of the nineteenth century be called the "alcoholic republic"?

8. In what ways did the admission of new states change the meaning of citizenship and suffrage?

GEOGRAPHY OBJECTIVES

1. Sketch the area of land, occupied by 1790, west of the Proclamation Line of 1763 (pp. 177, 267).

2. In what territories was most of the Indian fighting concentrated in the years after the Treaty of Paris (p. 262)?

3. Which states were the most densely populated in 1820? Which ones had grown the fastest since 1790 (p. 267)?

4. Name and locate the new slave states that entered the Union between 1790 and 1820 (p. 269).

SUGGESTED ESSAY TOPICS

1. In what ways did the American economy diversify during the first decades of the early republic? Discuss the impact of diversification on the economy of the different regions of the nation.

2. Explain the importance of gender roles in a patriarchal society. How did the role of women and men change in the course of the early republic?

3. In the years after the American Revolution, the country seemed to go in two opposite directions on the issue of slavery. Why did some sections of the country "recommit to slavery," while other regions gradually terminated the institution altogether? Why did Methodists fail in their attempts to spread John Wesley's message that slavery transgressed "all the laws of Justice, Mercy and Truth"?

SUGGESTED WEB ACTIVITY FOR THE CLASSROOM

Monticello: The Home of Thomas Jefferson

http://www.monticello.org/index.html

This site provides tours of Monticello. It contains sections on Jefferson, The House, The Plantation, The Grounds, and Resources. Some are virtual tours that require a variety of plug-ins to access. Navigating the site can be time-consuming, but it provides some extremely interesting 3-D views inside the house. Worth the effort.

LECTURE OUTLINE

1. The United States at the turn of the nineteenth century was a **farmer's republic,** composed of a rural people whose lives revolved around community and family. Few Americans lived in metropolitan areas or regularly engaged in market relations.

   (Show Transparency 7-01: Venerate the Plough)

   a. **Households** were a vital part of the economy, with women providing more diverse and dependable diets for their families and men performing most manual labor in the fields.

   b. Manufacturing depended heavily on **rural industry,** with families involved in shoemaking, furniture making, and various other manufactures which could be sold as well as serving their own families' needs.

   c. **Neighbors** proved especially important as sources of information, exchange, and assistance, as people relied on a system of barter and cooperation with their neighbors to fulfill their needs.

   d. Children still gained the wealth of their parents through **inheritance,** but the institution underwent dramatic changes in the early years of the new republic as owning land became problematic.

   e. Rising **standards of living** materially improved the lives of many Americans, while also increasing the disparity between rich and poor.

2. Americans flooded out of the East, continuing a constant emigration **from backcountry to frontier** that would last a century and bring them into conflict with Native Americans already there.

   a. The eventual eviction of the British from the continent, combined with Americans' insatiable appetite for western lands, virtually guaranteed the **destruction of the Woodlands Indians** in only a few decades at the end of the eighteenth and beginning of the nineteenth centuries.

   (Show Transparency 7-02: Map, Native America, 1783–1819)

   b. Despite the efforts of the likes of Alexander McGillivray, Tecumseh, and the Prophet to articulate some form of Indian cultural renewal, Indians could secure no real cooperation with or acceptance from the American nation.

   c. While remaining an area largely beyond effective government and organized institutions, the backcountry was transformed into a beckoning frontier by the flood of western settlers from 1790 to 1815.

   (Show Transparency 7-03: Map, Population Density, 1790–1820)

3. The **plantation South** underwent a similar transformation, as new settlers and new crops—cotton in particular—changed the character of much of the region from 1790 to 1820.

   a. Despite crop diversification in the Chesapeake that led to the manumission of more than 30,000 slaves, the institution of **slavery** became increasingly enmeshed in southern life during the first decades of the nineteenth century.

   b. The lower South made a particularly strong, if unpremeditated, **recommitment to slavery** after the development of the cotton gin, aided by the widespread purchase of slaves from the upper South.

   (Show Transparency 7-04: Map, Distribution of Slave Population, 1790–1820)

   c. Nowhere were the issues of **race, gender, and labor** more contested than in the Chesapeake, where the economic transition from tobacco to grain altered many social institutions and created a new division of labor.

    d. The areas of the Deep South where rice and indigo were the primary staples developed a **lowland task system** of slave labor in which slaves gained a significant amount of autonomy as well as separation from white masters.

4. **Seaport cities** grew and became the largest urban areas in the years 1790–1815, at the beginning of which only 6 percent of Americans lived in areas with a population over 2,500.

    a. **Commerce,** particularly the export of foodstuffs and the import of European products, fueled the steady growth of the urban centers along the Atlantic seaboard.

    b. **Poverty** was more visible in cities, where slums emerged as the self-contained neighborhoods of a growing indigent population that was being excluded from the new accumulation of wealth.

    c. The **status of labor** changed with the decline of the unique position of artisans, as a few became shop owners but most joined the growing pool of unskilled and semiskilled laborers.

5. The **assault on authority** and deference were characteristic features of the rise of a democratic society, one in which ordinary people would play a major role.

    a. Many contemporaries believed they were witnessing the declension of **paternal power,** as children chose their own marriage partners and depended on themselves to develop their futures, and the entire country seemed to celebrate youth.

    b. Americans drank such a high volume of intoxicating beverages, especially whiskey, that some have called the period an **alcoholic republic.**

    c. High literacy rates and the proliferation of reading materials, especially newspapers and novels, contributed to the **democratization of print** in the early republic.

    d. **Citizenship** remained the province of white males. The franchise expanded greatly to include virtually all white men, especially in the new western states, even as new restrictions ensured the disfranchisement of all women and blacks.

6. Americans embraced a form of **republican religion** that in many ways reflected the democratization of the polity.

    a. The most important feature of republican religion was the decline of **established churches** as the states withdrew their monetary support.

    b. The **rise of the democratic sects,** Baptists and Methodists especially, reflected Americans' desire to have choice and freedom in religion and to take responsibility for their own salvation.

    (Show Transparency 7-05: Map, Growth of American Methodism, 1775–1850)

    c. The **Christianization of the white South** featured great camp meetings of evangelical Protestants and the simultaneous growth of both black and white denominations of Baptists, Methodists, and Presbyterians.

    d. **Evangelicals and slavery** maintained a tenuous relationship, with evangelicals first supporting abolition but ultimately remaining subservient to the economic interests of the plantation South.

    e. The first decades of the nineteenth century witnessed the beginnings of **African-American Christianity** and religious institutions in which blacks attained autonomy from the dominant white society.

    f. **Gabriel's Rebellion** in Virginia was brutally subdued in the summer of 1800, but nonetheless expressed many slaves' concept of black republicanism, their own version of "natural rights."

Conclusion: Americans celebrated the beginning of national government in the 1790s as an overwhelmingly rural people. Yet the young nation experienced many changes that would usher in a more individualistic, acquisitive republic in the years to come. Transformations in the cultural life of the country accompanied economic agitation, as Americans contemplated the future prospects for their country.

FOCUS ON FEATURES

American Album: Revival at York, Pennsylvania, p. 282
History Through Film: *A Midwife's Tale*, p. 258
Link to the Past: Religion and the Founding of the American Republic (Library of Congress), p. 284

TEACHING RESOURCES

Lewis and Clark: The Journey of the Corps of Discovery is Ken Burns' rendition of the most famous American expedition of the nineteenth century. PBS Video (120 minutes each).

A Few Men Well-Conducted: The George Rogers Clark Story tells the epic story of courage on the frontier and the trek into the Kentucky and Illinois backcountry in the era of the American Revolution. Filmic Archives (23 minutes).

Settling the Old Northwest details the dynamics of settlement and socialization in the lands between the Ohio and Mississippi Rivers. Filmic Archives (18 minutes).

Thomas Jefferson: The Pursuit of Liberty attempts to give a balanced portrait of the man and his ideas. It explores the complex life of the man who simultaneously held slaves and authored the Declaration of Independence. Thomas Jefferson Memorial Foundation Video (38 minutes).

Awakening Land, based on the Conrad Richter trilogy, details the story of life on the Ohio frontier. PBS Video (108 minutes).

Chapter 8

COMPLETING THE REVOLUTION, 1789–1815

CHAPTER SUMMARY

When Robert Livingston swore in George Washington as America's first president on April 30, 1789, the American people had much to celebrate. They had won the war, secured independence, adopted a new government, and unanimously elected Washington their leader. Still, as the new president well understood, there was much to be done to complete the Revolution.

The first Federalist administration, together with the first Congress, boasted some of the country's "best and brightest." Complementing the president were Vice President John Adams of Massachusetts, Secretary of State Thomas Jefferson of Virginia, and Treasury Secretary Alexander Hamilton of New York. Consciously playing the role of president of a large and diverse nation, Washington assiduously sought to foster unity within the government. He judiciously distributed patronage to men from every state and himself made a tour of the North. Unanimously elected to a second term, Washington proved only marginally successful at keeping himself above factional disputes. No sooner had Hamilton issued his comprehensive economic reports, which included federal assumption of state war debts, funding the government's liabilities at 100 percent, and the creation of a national bank, than a fierce opposition emerged in the cabinet and in Congress. With the president's backing, Hamilton pressed ahead with his vision of a strong central government, while his opponents, coalescing around Jefferson and James Madison, fought vigorously against what they considered a travesty of the narrow language of the Constitution. When Washington retired at the end of his second term, he warned in vain against the dangers of party spirit and its potential for splitting the country.

Foreign affairs plagued the administration of John Adams. The French Revolution and the ensuing Anglo–French War split the country down the middle. President Adams heeded Washington's warning about foreign entanglements. He ignored the advice of the Democratic-Republicans who sympathized with France, as well as those in his own Federalist Party who urged him to declare war on the French. Through the XYZ Affair, the quasi-war, and the Alien and Sedition Acts controversy, Adams managed to keep the young nation at peace. Staying out of the war, in the end, irreparably damaged the Federalist Party as well as the president's political fortunes. Adams became the first chief executive to lose his bid for reelection.

Historians have called Jefferson's defeat of Adams the "Revolution of 1800." Not only was the campaign ferociously fought between rival parties with new electioneering techniques, but the election itself marked the first time in history that power was transferred peacefully from one party to another. Adams and the Federalists were not entirely confident that Jefferson would not destroy the Republic, but they well understood that he had been legally and constitutionally elected president. With the ouster of Adams, the Federalists could only rely on John Marshall, newly appointed Chief Justice of the Supreme Court, to preserve federalism in Washington.

Jefferson's policies as president reflected for the most part his vision of a small government in a large agrarian republic. Accordingly, he shrank the size of the bureaucracy and slashed spending for the standing army and navy. Then, in one bold stroke, he doubled the size of the nation. The Louisiana Purchase, while a heavy-handed executive motion, proved to be Jefferson's most important act as president. For $15 million, the president secured America's future as an "empire of liberty."

Like his predecessor, Jefferson found himself embroiled in foreign policy. At once curtailing the nascent United States navy, the president pursued an uncompromising policy toward both England and France. While nonimportation proved a failure and the 1807 embargo a fiasco, Jefferson did manage to leave office with the country at peace. His successor was not so fortunate. The War of 1812, which New Englanders derisively called "Mr. Madison's War," accomplished little besides getting the nation's capitol burned by the British. The Treaty of Ghent effectively ended the war where it had started, despite the Federalist debacle at the Hartford Convention. The war also witnessed the emergence of Andrew Jackson as the hero of the Battle of New Orleans. Although the battle took place more than two weeks after the war had ended, Jackson emerged as America's first prominent national figure not associated directly with the Revolution. As a result of the War of 1812, the Democratic-Republicans vanquished the Federalists, but at a price. In fighting the great conflagration, they reluctantly had adopted most of their opponent's policies. Protecting liberty required the use of power.

LIBERTY, EQUALITY, POWER: A THEMATIC BRAID

Completing the Revolution, most Americans agreed, required the creation of a new national government. The Constitutional Convention created a government with vastly greater powers than those Congress had enjoyed under the Articles of Confederation. Early in George Washington's presidency, however, deep divisions appeared between those who felt the Constitution set limits on central power and those who considered the Constitution a blueprint for expanded governmental action. In the early Republic, the century-long fight between power and liberty continued under the new guise of Federalist versus Democratic-Republican.

Federalists believed that power ensured liberty. Accordingly, they sought to engage the government actively in creating a powerful commercial republic, based on internal economic development, overseas trade, and a navy strong enough to defend American interests. If these actions entailed a loose construction of the Constitution and reliance on the "necessary and proper" clause, then so be it.

Republicans, including James Madison, the "father of the Constitution," feared power in anyone's hands. They were convinced that Federalists would come to abuse central power just as the British, whom their opponents emulated, had done in the decades before the Revolution. For Republicans, completing the Revolution meant ensuring liberty through a bill of rights, strict construction of the Constitution, and a vigilant stand against their power-hungry opponents. Ironically, Republicans and Federalists agreed on the meaning of equality. Americans were hardly equal, nor should they be. Equality rested solely in those independent members of society who had a visible financial stake in the country. This proved to be a minority of predominantly white males.

IDENTIFICATIONS

Federalist Party	Democratic-Republicans
precedent	James Madison
Bill of Rights	Judiciary Act of 1789
presidential cabinet	Alexander Hamilton
John Jay	Report on Public Credit
Bank of the United States	Whiskey Rebellion
strict construction	French Revolution
Citizen Genêt	orders in council
Pinckney's Treaty	Washington's Farewell Address
XYZ Affair	Alien and Sedition Acts
Virginia and Kentucky Resolves	High Federalists
John Marshall	midnight appointments

Aaron Burr
Louisiana Purchase
Yazoo Land Company
Haiti
Napoleon Bonaparte
Fort Mims Massacre
Chesapeake–Leopard affair
Battle of the Thames
Hartford Convention

District of Columbia
John Randolph
Marbury v. *Madison*
"empire of liberty"
Non-Importation Act
War Hawks
Francis Scott Key
Oliver Hazard Perry

CHRONOLOGY

1789   Washington inaugurated as first president of the United States in New York City.
Judiciary Act establishes a Supreme Court.

1790   Hamilton's Report on Public Credit delivered to Congress.
Bill of Rights drafted by Congress.

1792   French Republic proclaimed.

1793   Anglo–French War.

1794   Whiskey Rebellion.
Jay's Treaty and Pinckney's Treaty ratified.
John Adams elected president.
Washington delivers his Farewell Address.

1798   XYZ Affair.
Undeclared war between the United States and France.
Alien and Sedition Acts passed by Congress.

1799   Slave revolution in Haiti.

1800   Washington, D.C., becomes American capital.
Republican Jefferson defeats Federalist Adams.

1803   Louisiana Territory purchased from France.
Marbury v. *Madison* case establishes judicial review.

1804   Twelfth Amendment to the Constitution.

1806   Non-Importation Act.

1807   Chesapeake–Leopard affair.
Congress passes Jefferson's Embargo Act.

1810   Macon's Bill No. 2.

1811   Henry Clay elected Speaker of the House.

1812–1814   War of 1812.

1814   Hartford Convention.
Treaty of Ghent.

1815   American victory in the Battle of New Orleans.

THEMATIC TOPICS FOR ENRICHMENT

1. What were the different titles suggested for the American president? Why did the debate prove so vitriolic?

2. Who was likely to be a Federalist? A Democratic-Republican?

3. List the specific liberties guaranteed in the Bill of Rights.

4. Explain the main points of Hamilton's economic plans.

5. Who were the members of Washington's first cabinet? What were their home states?

6. Assess Hamilton's and Jefferson's views on the constitutionality of the Bank of the United States.

7. Explain why the Jeffersonians sympathized with France and the Federalists sided with England in the 1790s.

8. What were the warnings Washington delivered in his Farewell Address? How well do you feel Americans have heeded what he had to say?

9. What were the Virginia and Kentucky Resolves written in response to? What was the basic principle behind them?

10. What was so important about New Orleans that Jefferson insisted that the United States gain control of the city?

11. Why did virtually all Federalists in the twelfth Congress vote against going to war with England in 1812? Assess the Federalist claim that the conflict was solely a "war of territorial aggression."

GEOGRAPHY OBJECTIVES

1. On a map of the United States in 1790, mark off the home states of the members of Washington's first cabinet (p. 298).

2. Identify the states that voted Republican and those that voted Federalist in the presidential election of 1800 (p. 304).

3. Mark on a map the major battles of the War of 1812 (p. 317).

4. Find the three United States capitals between 1789 and 1800 (p. 317).

SUGGESTED ESSAY TOPICS

1. In what ways did the fight between the Federalists and the Democratic-Republicans echo the Revolutionary contest between liberty and power?

2. What did Jefferson mean in his inaugural address of 1801 when he claimed that "we are all Republicans, we are all Federalists"? Assess the importance of the "peaceful transit of power" after the election of 1800.

3. How well did Thomas Jefferson live up to his own political ideals of less government and "strict constructionism" during his two terms in the presidency?

4. Describe the foreign policies of the Federalists and those of the Republicans and compare the two. Which were more effective?

5. Read "Federalist #10" by James Madison and answer the following questions: What is it about? Has the Constitution succeeded in checking the danger of majority factions as the author believed it would?

6. Compare and contrast the presidential administrations of George Washington and Thomas Jefferson, both in regard to domestic matters and to foreign affairs. Discuss the attitudes and beliefs of both men about the proper course for the country to follow.

SUGGESTED WEB ACTIVITY FOR THE CLASSROOM

Lewis and Clark Web site.

http://www.pbs.org/lewisandclark/

Visitors to this site can click on an interactive game based on the Lewis and Clark journals. "Into the Unknown" allows participants to make decisions based on items from the Corps of Discovery leaders' journal entries. Other segments also prove informative and entertaining.

LECTURE OUTLINE

1. **Establishing the government** and giving it the ability to tackle the nation's economic and political problems was the first priority for Washington, his administration, and the first Congress.

    a. The Washington administration, in order to build a stable government, accepted the irony of appearing to create a **"republican court"** of powerful appointed officials in the interest of a democratic society.

    b. Leadership in the **first Congress** fell to James Madison, under whose guidance the Congress pursued a course to strengthen federal authority over the states.

        i. The **Bill of Rights** became the instrument that did the most to ease fear of federal power.

        ii. Madison also oversaw the creation of the **executive departments.**

   (Show Transparency 8-01: The Congressional Brawlers, 1798)

    c. The cornerstone of the first Washington administration was the system of **Hamiltonian economics** that would begin to regulate the currency, foster economic expansion, and sanction an ongoing national debt as the cornerstone of a powerful state.

    d. Several aspects of the plan of Hamiltonian economics were reminiscent of English practices, especially his proposals for establishing a **national bank** and enacting **excise taxes.**

    e. The **rise of opposition** was inevitable, as southerners especially felt that Hamilton's plans favored the commercial interests of the North.

    f. The beginnings of party politics stemmed from the growing rift between Washington's two principal advisors in the cabinet, **Jefferson and Hamilton.**

2. Foreign policy concerns often cast a shadow over domestic concerns, as the nation's political leaders differed greatly in their views on the ongoing **war between France and England** to 1800.

    a. Most Americans initially considered **the French Revolution** to be a significant step toward a republican world, but Federalists soon came to view the events in France with skepticism, fear, and dismay.

    b. **Citizen Genêt,** as French minister to the United States in 1793, conspicuously intervened in American internal affairs, while Britain stepped up its questionable tactics against American ships on the high seas.

    c. The Washington administration faced acute **western troubles** in the course of 1794, ultimately sending an army of 12,000 men to quell the most troublesome incident, the so-called Whiskey Rebellion in Pennsylvania.

   (Show Transparency 8-02: Map, Securing the West, 1790–1796)

    d. Vehemently opposed by many, the **Jay Treaty** helped the United States avert war with England, though it settled few of the issues left unresolved in the Revolutionary War settlement.

    e. In September 1796, newspapers printed **Washington's Farewell Address,** in which the chief executive announced his retirement and offered several admonitions about politics and foreign policy.

    f.   In a case of early electoral college intrigue, John Adams, the heir apparent, narrowly defeated Thomas Jefferson in the **election of 1796,** winning New England and several of the middle states.

    g.   **Troubles with France** plagued Adams's entire administration.

    h.   The struggle with France and England turned into a **crisis at home from 1798 to 1800** especially when the Federalist Congress passed the Alien and Sedition Acts and the Kentucky and Virginia legislatures sought to nullify them within their state boundaries.

    i.   Politicians fought heatedly over development of the **United States Army,** including questions about the best fighting size and leadership.

    j.   The **election of 1800** marked the first defeat of an incumbent administration as well as the peaceful transfer of power from one party to another, despite an electoral tie that had thrown the question into the Congress.

3. Making good on their campaign pledges, the **Jeffersonians in power** immediately sought to curtail the pomp and ceremony so prominent in the previous administrations.

    a.   While it continued many of the features of its predecessors, the **Republican program** articulated by Jefferson sought to shrink the activities of the central government and to eliminate altogether the national debt.

    b.   For Jefferson, **cleansing the government** meant the removal of inept partisan opponents while shrinking the size and cost of the government.

    c.   The greatest disputes of the administration proved to be between the **Jeffersonians and the courts.**

        i.   Republicans led by John Randolph sought **the impeachments of John Pickering and Samuel Chase** for a combination of partisanship and gross dereliction of duty.

        ii. **Justice Marshall's court**—and Chief Justice Marshall himself—proved to be Jefferson's greatest challenge, particularly after Marshall's momentous decision that established judicial review in the case of *Marbury v. Madison* in 1803.

    d.   Jefferson secured his legacy and his reelection with the remarkable purchase of **Louisiana** from the French in 1803 for the moderate sum of fifteen million dollars.

(Show Transparency 8-03: Map, Louisiana Purchase)

4. America's attention in the coming years remained riveted on the emerging crisis between the United States and Europe, as the nation debated involvement in the **Napoleonic Wars** of 1804 to 1815.

    a.   Jefferson and Madison understood the daunting **dilemmas of neutrality** in a world at war but had a great deal of difficulty convincing New Englanders that neutrality should be maintained at all costs.

    b.   The president desperately tried to steer clear of the **trouble on the high seas** created by both British and French naval depredations and the British practice of impressing American sailors into service on their undermanned ships.

    c.   Jefferson sought to avoid war in the last years of his presidency through the passage of the **Embargo Act of 1807,** which proved extremely unpopular in New England since it crippled American commerce.

    d.   Jefferson's retirement and the failure of the embargo seemed to send the country inevitably down the **road to war** with Great Britain.

    e.   Led by Henry Clay of Kentucky, the **War Hawk Congress of 1811–1812** pushed for war with England in order to settle a number of unresolved issues, not the least of which was Britain's influence with the Indians in the West.

f. Despite strong opposition by Federalists, the Republicans of the South and West led a divided country into the **War of 1812,** determined to prove their sovereignty to Great Britain.

(Show Transparency 8-04: Map, War of 1812)

   i. Early skirmishes included a failed northern invasion as part of the War with Canada in 1812–1813 that included depredations on both sides amid a growing sense of solidarity among British Canadian settlers.
   ii. **Tecumseh** made his last stand for the British at the Thames River on October 5, 1813, where Richard M. Johnson claimed to have fatally wounded the warrior.
   iii. The **British offensive of 1814** included the humiliating sacking of the nation's capital and Andrew Jackson's smashing victory over General Packenham's army after the war had officially ended.
   iv. A group of disgruntled Federalists gathered at the **ill-fated Hartford Convention** to protest publicly "Mr. Madison's War," but they had no real effect since the war was over.
   v. The war officially ended with the signing of the **Treaty of Ghent** on December 23, 1814, though the treaty did nothing but end the fighting between the two sides, leaving other matters unsettled.

Conclusion: Almost all of the founding generation agreed that the stronger national government ushered in by the Constitution was essential to American prosperity and security. Even Thomas Jefferson, by the time he retired to Monticello after the War of 1812, was ready to agree that there was, indeed, a place for the manufacturer in America. No longer could he argue that America could maintain its state of isolation with a nation comprised solely of yeomen farmers. He and other republicans still believed that "he who governs best, governs least," but they had faced the reality that some Federalist programs had merit.

FOCUS ON FEATURES

American Album: The Capital of the Republic, p. 296
History Through Film: *The Buccaneer*, p. 320
Link to the Past: Congressional Debates, p. 293

TEACHING RESOURCES

Thomas Jefferson is Ken Burns's fine two-part examination of the third president, with Sam Waterston reading Jefferson's words. PBS Video (180 minutes total).

United States vs. Aaron Burr re-creates the trial of Burr, the one-time vice president of the United States. Educational Video (60 minutes).

The Life of George Washington features Bill Bradley narrating a detailed portrait of the first president of the United States. Filmic Archives (32 minutes).

City Out of the Wilderness: Washington details the founding of the American capital at the end of the eighteenth century. Filmic Archives (30 minutes).

Virginia Plantations focuses on two of Virginia's most famous homes, Monticello and Mount Vernon. Filmic Archives (30 minutes).

Marbury v. *Madison*, one tape in the *Equal Justice Under Law* series, explains this 1803 Supreme Court case and its significance for American jurisprudence. PBS Video (30 minutes).

Mr. Jefferson and His University examines the originality of Jefferson's vision through an examination of the University of Virginia and several of his other achievements. Films for the Humanities (52 minutes).

Chapter 9

THE MARKET REVOLUTION, 1815–1860

CHAPTER SUMMARY

The conclusion of the War of 1812 ushered in a new economic era. Between 1815 and the coming of the Civil War, the United States underwent a furious economic transformation. The primary engines of this great expansion of the United States' economy proved to be a revolution in transportation and the subsequent burgeoning of a market economy. Jefferson's republic of independent farmers became, over the course of several decades, a market-oriented capitalist society.

It is ironic that the Republican-dominated Fourteenth Congress devised the nationalistic programs that helped to subsidize the market revolution. In 1816, Congress chartered the Second Bank of the United States and enacted a protective tariff that raised rates an average of 25 percent. It also passed several bills to provide federal money for roads, canals, and other internal improvements. Although Congress never embraced Henry Clay's "American System" in its entirety, the Republican government assumed a significant share of the burden for improving the nation's transportation system.

Both states and private investors contributed ideas and capital to the transportation revolution. New York entrepreneur Robert Fulton launched the first steamboat in 1807. In the ensuing years, a proliferation of steamboats enabled farmers to make their way speedily back upriver after selling their products. What formerly was a two- to three-month trip from New Orleans to Louisville or Cincinnati became a pleasant ten-day river ride by 1850.

The Erie Canal turned out to be one of the greatest achievements of the transportation revolution. Built between 1817 and 1825, the 364-mile canal connected the Great Lakes to New York City. It generated huge profits for its investors, turned upstate New York wilderness into highly desirable farmland, drew many New Englanders and immigrants westward, and enabled New York to live up to its billing as the Empire State. Eventually displaced by the railroads, the Erie Canal remained the crowning achievement of the early years of the transportation revolution.

The Federalists had long held that federal power could ensure the growth of a market economy. John Marshall, as the sole Federalist in a prominent position in the national government at the time, used the Supreme Court to prove the Federalists right. In a series of court cases, Marshall established the supremacy of the federal government, ensured the sanctity of charters and contracts, and set interstate commerce outside the regulation of the individual states. By the time Marshall retired in 1835, the Supreme Court had guaranteed that the United States would enjoy the benefits of a national economic system.

By far the most important result of the market revolution was the steady rise in material standards of living. Improved transportation, lower freight costs, expanded overseas markets, and the rise of a cash-based economy all contributed to American prosperity. Still, the market revolution did not come cheap. Many people failed to prosper in the generally improving national economy, while others systematically were excluded from enjoying the ever-increasing profits from their labors. As cotton production and profits boomed in the South, more and more slaves suffered from the arduous demands of the cotton economy. When the price of slaves increased, fewer Chesapeake slaveholders freed their slaves. In no small measure, the first manumission ended with Eli Whitney's invention of the cotton gin. The market revolution did not, as some had hoped, signal the end of slavery.

LIBERTY, EQUALITY, POWER: A THEMATIC BRAID

Liberty, equality, and power are not solely functions of governmental and legal action. Economic factors have proven as important as any others in Americans' pursuit of progress toward greater personal liberty and equality. The market revolution provided a tremendous opportunity for Americans to stake their claim to the ideals of the American Revolution and independence. Material standards of living rose significantly in the years after the War of 1812.

Even then not everyone benefited equally. Some grew wealthy, others improved their lives somewhat, and still others found their lives adversely affected by the growth of American capitalism. Transportation usually proved critical. For those Americans who could farm, mine, build, or otherwise produce items for a market, fortunes generally improved, sometimes dramatically, during the first half of the nineteenth century. For those who found themselves unable to produce anything for market consumption, few economic opportunities appeared. Without skills or capital, many Americans joined a growing class of workers and laborers, who, except for slaves, occupied the lowest station in society.

In sum, then, as the United States became a world economic power, the material wealth of its citizens grew apace. With prosperity came more opportunity and financial freedom, yet the nation did not become a land of equality of opportunity. The market revolution proved a mixed blessing. As American wealth increased, so did the gap between rich and poor. By the middle of the nineteenth century, Jefferson's idealistic vision of an egalitarian society of free farmers and artisans was buried under a burgeoning capitalist society.

IDENTIFICATIONS

Treaty of Ghent

second Bank of the United States

John C. Calhoun

internal improvements

Dartmouth College v. *Woodward*

McCulloch v. *Maryland*

Baltimore and Ohio Railroad

Robert Fulton

Natchez Trace

cash-crop business

McCormick reaper

Richard Arkwright

Frederick Law Olmsted

paternalism

Battle of New Orleans

"American System"

Tariff of 1816

National Road

Erie Canal

Gibbons v. *Ogden*

Lancaster Turnpike

DeWitt Clinton

Main Line Canal

Peter Cartwright

Farmer's Almanac

Boston Associates

Waltham System

CHRONOLOGY

1790	Samuel Slater constructs Arkwright spinning mill.
1801	John Marshall appointed Chief Justice of Supreme Court.
1807	Robert Fulton launches the *Clermont*, first steamboat, on its maiden trip.
1813	Boston Associates builds first mill in Waltham, Massachusetts.
1815	End of the War of 1812.

1816	Congress charters Second Bank of the United States.
	McCulloch v. *Maryland*.
	Revised protective tariff passed by Congress.
1818	National Road completed as far west as Wheeling, Virginia.
1819–1825	New York builds Erie Canal between the Hudson River and Buffalo.
1822	President Monroe vetoes National Road reparations bill.
1824	*Gibbons* v. *Ogden*.
1828	Baltimore and Ohio Railroad begins full operation.
1835	Main Line Canal connects Philadelphia and Pittsburgh.

THEMATIC TOPICS FOR ENRICHMENT

1. What was Henry Clay's "American System"?
2. Explain the specific legal results of the three Marshall decisions handed down between 1816 and 1824.
3. What was so important about the invention of steamboats for American transportation in the early republic?
4. Why was the transportation revolution so important to the opening of a market economy in early America?
5. Was any one region of the country mostly excluded from the burgeoning national market system? Explain.
6. Evaluate the role of the plantation on the economic development of the South.
7. In what ways were New England farmers adversely affected by the market revolution?

GEOGRAPHY OBJECTIVES

1. Trace the route of the Erie Canal across New York. From how far inland could goods be transported by water to New York City after the completion of the canal (p. 330)?
2. Through which states did the National, or Cumberland, Road make its way (p. 330)?
3. Find the path of the "Natchez Trace" north from New Orleans through Mississippi (p. 330).
4. Compare the rates of travel from New York City to points inland in 1800 and 1830 (p. 332).
5. In which sections of the country were the greatest miles of railroads laid (p. 323)?
6. Contrast the regional growth of cotton in 1801 and 1859 (p. 348).

SUGGESTED ESSAY TOPICS

1. In what ways did the market revolution shatter Jefferson's vision of an agrarian republic?
2. What was the transportation revolution? Discuss the main features of its development between 1815 and 1860.
3. How did the decisions of the Marshall Court demonstrate Marshall's conviction that "a natural and beneficial link exists between federal power and market society"?

© 2002 Thomson Learning, Inc.

SUGGESTED WEB ACTIVITY FOR THE CLASSROOM

Time Table of the Lowell Mills

http://www.library.csi.cuny.edu/dept/americanstudies/lavender/graphics/ttable.jpg

This site contains an actual schedule from the Lowell Mills for 1853–1854. The table contains some items that should be surprising to students and which should serve as a good introduction to a discussion of workers' rights then and now.

LECTURE OUTLINE

1. The party of Jefferson changed dramatically in the years after his retirement. Republicans increasingly agreed that **government and markets** must work closely together to foster the country's economic expansion and independence from Europe.

   a. Henry Clay's **"American System"** included the charter of the second **Bank of the United States** in 1816 over the objections of a steadily increasing number of Republicans who viewed it as unconstitutional.

   b. **"The American System"** incorporated an elaborate system of **tariffs and internal improvements** that expressed Clay's belief that the government must be used for progressive purposes.

   c. Politicians and lawyers sought to assure the effective interaction of **markets and the law,** as reflected in a series of important Marshall Supreme Court decisions and various state court cases as well.

2. The **transportation revolution** proved critical to national economic development because the price of many commodities depended more on the costs associated with transporting them to market than on those of production.

   a. The means of **transportation** had not changed very dramatically for many years; a rudimentary system of roads barely supplemented river travel.

      i. Technology and changes in laws resulted in dramatic improvements in **roads and rivers** as means of transportation, with the steamboat being the development that made agriculture in the interior productive.

      ii. Improvements in **canals and railroads** augured a wholesale change in the means of transport in the United States, despite their high costs.

      (Show Transparency 9-02: Map, Rivers, Roads, and Canals, 1825–1860)

   b. The transportation revolution resulted in a dramatic reduction in the **time and money** it took to transport bulk commodities.

   c. Improved transportation also meant the growth of specific **markets and regions** in an economy of scale, with the West and Northeast more successful in this process of integration than the South.

3. The advent of cash markets ushered in the transformation from **yeoman to businessman,** particularly in the rural North and West.

   a. Cash-oriented farms proved instrumental in shaping the **northern landscape,** as farmers sought to exploit urban demand for perishable crops.

   b. The **transformation of rural outwork** into more market-oriented production had consequences for both the economy and for society in general.

   c. With the shift to specialized market agriculture, much of the North and West witnessed the growth of **farmers as consumers.**

    d. The Northwest became home to many **southern migrants** who rejected slavery but maintained strong ties to southern cultural traditions.

    e. The Northwest was also the destination of myriad **northern migrants** who rapidly embraced most agricultural improvements in order to maximize their cash-crop harvests.

    f. No institution changed more dramatically than **households,** which shifted from economic production to raising fewer children and preparing them for a career outside the home, redefining housework, and expanding privacy and comfort.

    g. New neighborhoods designed as a **landscape of privacy** ushered out the old practices and forms of neighborliness characteristic of communities where everyone knew everybody else.

4. **The Industrial Revolution** began in New England in the 1830s and 1840s.

    a. Factory towns under the **Rhode Island system** emerged as a result initially of the industrial espionage of Richard Arkwright, who stole English plans for a textile machine.

    b. Factory towns under the **Waltham system** employed young, single women in their mills, exploiting this readily available source of cheap labor, in the process changing many of their lives forever.

    c. Cities featured the growth of a class of **urban businessmen** who used their wealth and position to dominate much of urban society.

    d. **Metropolitan industrialization** sparked the development of a new middle class that made the old distinction between proprietor and dependent obsolete.

5. Proponents of the **market revolution in the South** based the need for such changes on westward expansion and the world's seemingly insatiable demand for cotton.

    (Show Transparency 9-03: Map, Cotton Production, 1801 and 1859)

    a. The huge profits from cotton planting necessitated the **organization of slave labor** into distinct strata, including the use of women in the fields and the encouragement of slave families.

    b. Planters used a system of **paternalism**—caring for slaves as more than mere property—to discourage the most vicious treatment of blacks and to ensure that the supply of slaves would not wane.

    c. With the economies of scale brought about by cotton production, southern society was increasingly split into a dual economy of **yeomen and planters.**

    d. Yeomen farmers generally had little interaction with **the market** dominated by the planters, concentrating instead mostly on subsistence agriculture and trade among themselves.

    e. **Plantations and southern development** went hand in hand; the southern economy grew rapidly, albeit narrowly, as a few planters churned profits back into land and slave labor, and most southerners remained on the fringes of that society.

Conclusion: Despite the fact that the Jeffersonians attempted to foster an agrarian republic of yeomen farmers, the War of 1812 and the strength of the American economy forced the Republican Party to adapt. Under Jefferson and Madison, Republicans endorsed many of the programs and initiatives that they had condemned under their Federalist predecessors. The nation was undergoing a transformation that signaled a burgeoning capitalistic market revolution, and despite southern reluctance to accept the facts, northern manufacturing was forcing the South into a subservient position.

FOCUS ON FEATURES

American Album: The Making of Rural Respectability, p. 334
History Through Film: *Gone with the Wind*, p. 352
Link to the Past: Lowell National Historic Park, p. 344

TEACHING RESOURCES

Remaking Society in the New Nation examines the struggles of two men who make their way in the early
years of the American republic. Filmic Archives (21 minutes).

The Louisiana Purchase: Moving West of the Mississippi highlights the politics and culture of the newest
settlements of turn-of-the-nineteenth-century America. Filmic Archives (16 minutes).

Settling the Old Northwest depicts the conflicts that arose between aggressive western settlers and the Native
American tribes between the Ohio and Mississippi Rivers. Filmic Archives (18 minutes).

Gone West exposes the harsh realities of life on the western frontier in the eras of Jefferson and Jackson.
BBC/Time-Life Video (52 minutes).

Chapter 10

TOWARD AN AMERICAN CULTURE

CHAPTER SUMMARY

New territories, the market revolution, and the continued spread of plantation slavery produced wave after wave of social change in America after 1815. New social patterns replaced or changed old ones, often as a consequence of religious revival. Americans remained primarily devoted to Protestantism, capitalism, and republican values, but the emerging northern middle class interpreted these matters differently than did the plantation owners of the South. In addition, northern urban workers, farmers, and free blacks defined these values differently among themselves. From these differences there emerged an American range of subcultures created by religion, region, class, and race.

Revivalists such as Charles Grandison Finney launched a new wave of evangelism that stressed individual salvation and social reform. They believed that such changes would trigger the millennium, a thousand-year reign of Christianity that would precede the Second Coming of Christ. The northern middle class responding to the evangelicals' crusade used this religious goal to create a culture based on a greatly altered family structure as well as on community moral reform.

Middle-class evangelism forever altered the American domestic arena. Gender determined the sphere of work to be done: Men went out of the home to work in markets and finance, while women maintained the household, made domestic life their domain, and assumed most of the child-rearing duties. In the sentimental literature that accompanied and exalted this domestic alteration, mothers became lay evangelicals who embodied correct Christian living and passed moral values on to their children.

Farmers, laborers, and other "plain people" of the North, in contrast, spurned middle-class optimism and reformism and maintained their simple faith in Providence. Many came to believe that Christ's Second Coming was at hand and found signs of this in nature's storms, eclipses, and shooting stars, as well as in man-made economic catastrophes. William Miller's predictions in the 1830s and 1840s convinced thousands that the world was about to end.

Concern that the patriarchal family was collapsing played a major role in the teachings of Joseph Smith. In the Book of Mormon, patriarchy is the ideal family organization and the villains are selfish merchants, lawyers, and evil priests. The Church of Jesus Christ of Latter-Day Saints, which Smith founded in 1830, established a lay hierarchy of adult males that ran the institution and ensured that believers continued to turn to a patriarchal government for the family and the community.

Greatly disturbing to the religious subcultures was the rise of a largely urban popular culture that revolved around young unmarried males. These men formed militia units, volunteer fire companies, and similar organizations that glorified drinking, boasting, and physical exploits. Blood sports such as cockfighting, dogfighting, and boxing attracted them. New types of entertainment in theaters drew them as well, where the boisterous, sometimes violent, patrons demanded coarse American drama filled with melodramatic themes, rather than the usual staid fare. The most popular of these theatrical offerings was the minstrel show, where performers in blackface poked fun at black dialect and folkways. Cheap novels and the "penny press" entertained the same patrons with lurid accounts of murder, mayhem, and sexual misconduct.

Meanwhile, white southerners remained localistic and culturally conservative. With a strong sense of family history, they fiercely guarded the traditional family structure and their own roles in it. Honor and reputation were everything, with the code of honor maintaining rigid distinctions between men and women, whites and blacks. "Southern life was not about freedom, individual fulfillment, or social progress; it was about honoring the obligations to which one was born."

A wave of revivalism at the beginning of the century stressed individual conversion more than social reform, and local control of religious matters rather than denominational directives. Churches thus became the most important institution in southern communities and controlled the moral life of their members much more than did the local government. By 1860, southern church members were overwhelmingly Methodists, Baptists, or Disciples of Christ.

In this social structure revolving around religion, family, and fixed social roles, slaves sought a better place for themselves. Their most prized privilege was to make and maintain a family; their greatest fear was separation from the family. Beyond the family, Christianity gave some slaves a sense of themselves as a historical people who, someday, would be delivered from bondage. America was the new Egypt, and Moses was the biblical figure most admired.

For some southern blacks, Christianity offered apocalyptic promises that led to revolt and a violent end to slavery. Denmark Vesey's planned revolt in 1822 equated Charleston with Jericho and South Carolina with Egypt, and in Nat Turner's 1831 revolt, Turner's religious visions served as a means to recruit fellow rebels and as a justification for slaughter.

LIBERTY, EQUALITY, POWER: A THEMATIC BRAID

Power for the northern middle class increasingly became attached to the conversion of others—not only to Christianity, but also to their own moral code. Moral reform became the means to achieve this power. For southern plantation owners, power meant not change, but the maintenance of the traditional family and the patriarchal class structure that separated men from women and whites from blacks. For the urban working class, power lay in the creation of their own organizations—volunteer fire companies and sporting clubs, for example—and the expansion of a crude, boisterous popular culture. Slaves in the South found few ways to exercise power except through the rare slave revolt.

Liberty and equality for whites in both North and South remained a racial prerogative based on republican values formulated in earlier eras. White women gained a measure of power and equality through the domesticity of home life and the resultant male sentimentalism of such. The female sphere defined by the home gave women more autonomy and greater social importance as the child raisers, moral teachers, and guardians. With the father absent more and more from the domestic scene, the mother's importance to the family greatly increased.

IDENTIFICATIONS

Middle class

Charles Grandison Finney

Sunday schools

millennialism

Ralph Waldo Emerson

Herman Melville

Walt Whitman

Uncle Tom's Cabin

Niagara Falls

Thomas Cole

southern code of honor

Seventh-Day Adventists

Book of Mormon

evangelicalism

blood sports

sentimentality

minstrel show

Nathaniel Hawthorne

penny press

Harriet Beecher Stowe

Denmark Vesey

Quaker City

Nat Turner

Joseph Smith

camp meeting

William Miller

CHRONOLOGY

1822	Denmark Vesey slave revolt plans exposed in Charleston, South Carolina.
1828	Alexander Campbell debates Robert Owen on religious piety in Cincinnati, Ohio.
1830	Charles G. Finney leads religious revival in Rochester, New York.
	Joseph Smith publishes the Book of Mormon and founds the Church of Jesus Christ of Latter-Day Saints.
1831	Mount Auburn Cemetery opens in Boston.
	First minstrel show is presented.
	Nat Turner's slave revolt breaks out in Virginia.
1835	Landscape artist Thomas Cole publishes "Essay on American Scenery."
1836	Emerson begins writing career with publication of *Nature*.
1837	Hawthorne publishes his first collection of stories, *Twice-Told Tales*.
1843–1844	William Miller converts thousands to the belief that the world is about to end.
1845	George Lippard's lurid novel *Quaker City* becomes a huge best-seller.
1849	Theater riot in New York City leaves twenty dead.
1851	Melville publishes *Moby Dick*.
1852	Harriet Beecher Stowe's antislavery novel *Uncle Tom's Cabin* is published to great popularity and controversy.
1853	Henry David Thoreau's *Walden* appears.
1856	Whitman publishes first editions of *Leaves of Grass*.

THEMATIC TOPICS FOR ENRICHMENT

1. How did the northern middle class's perceptions of Christianity differ from those of the "plain people"?
2. Explain the rise of domesticity and sentimentalism. How did women benefit from the new definition of their roles?
3. Discuss the changes in Americans' appreciation of the fine arts. How did their view of nature change?
4. Define the "popular culture" that arose among unmarried, urban males in the early decades of the nineteenth century. What role did immigrants play in this transformation?
5. Discuss the religious beliefs and social philosophy of southern plantation owners and their families.
6. Discuss how southerners used Christianity to justify the enslavement of blacks.

GEOGRAPHY OBJECTIVES

1. Compare the growth of cities north of the Mason–Dixon Line with that of cities in the southern states (p. 330).
2. Find the locations of the Denmark Vesey affair and the Nat Turner rebellion (p. 348).
3. Locate the birthplaces of Emerson, Hawthorne, Thoreau, Melville, and Whitman (p. 298).

SUGGESTED ESSAY TOPICS

1. Define the term "middle class" and discuss the factors that led to its growth in the early nineteenth century.

2. What is a religious revival? In what ways did religion figure into the lives of Americans in the first half of the 1800s?

3. What were the key features in the development of American literary culture in the decades before the Civil War?

4. Compare and contrast the cultures of the North and the South in the first half of the 1800s.

5. Explain the slaves' interpretation of religion and family. Did Christianity help or hamper slaves in dealing with their condition? Explain.

SUGGESTED WEB ACTIVITY FOR THE CLASSROOM

Godey's Lady's Book

  http://www.history.rochester.edu/godeys/

This site contains samples of the first mass circulation periodical in the United States aimed at women. Students should enjoy taking a look at the life of "ladies" of that era.

LECTURE OUTLINE

1. A great development of the first part of the nineteenth century was the advent of a distinct **northern middle class** of Protestant business-oriented folk who came to dominate northern culture.

    a. Members of the middle class attended church regularly, emerging from a solid **evangelical base** of Christian revivalism that encouraged their economic success.

    b. The **cult of domesticity** resulted from the middle-class distinction between private home and public work and politics, with the latter the exclusive domain of men.

    c. The popular literature of the class, such as *Godey's Lady's Book*, featured effusive **sentimentality** directed primarily at women, while Harriet Beecher Stowe's *Uncle Tom's Cabin* in effect used that sentimentality to indict slavery.

    d. Americans slowly came to view the **fine arts** as something that could take on a non-European, indigenous character, one that glorified their conquest of nature.

    e. Americans began to incorporate **nature into their art,** and to incorporate artistic elements into their natural surroundings.

    f. Improved transportation made **scenic tourism** a special American form of entertainment, with Niagara Falls one of the country's most popular destinations.

2. **The plain people of the North,** often denied a chance to experience middle-class values, rejected much of the sentimentality and evangelicalism of those values and pursued their own distinct forms of culture instead.

    a. The **religion of the common folk** proved far less sentimental and far more submissive than that of the middle class.

    b. **Popular millennialism,** particularly that of William Miller and the Millerites, looked forward to God's imminent arrival to redeem the saved.

    c. Some religious ideologies appealed to the notions that **family and society** must hold the line against encroaching and immoral market forces.

    d.   The **prophet Joseph Smith,** after the angel Moroni appeared to him in a vision in 1827, articulated a version of American Protestantism known as Mormonism, which reestablished a patriarchal hierarchy for home and religious life.

3.   The **rise of popular culture** in America accompanied the profusion of religious institutions.

    a.   Drinking, fighting, and **blood sports** such as cockfighting, ratting, and dogfights proved highly popular with the urban working class.

    b.   Prizefighting, or **boxing,** grew out of this subterranean culture to become a highly popular form of entertainment throughout society.

    c.   Americans of all social classes began to patronize the **American theater,** which featured everything from Shakespeare to amateur spectacles, with performers sometimes accompanied by rowdiness and even violence.

    d.   The most popular form of theater among males was the blackface **minstrel show,** which demonstrated the blatant racism of most of America.

    e.   Among the many commodities the market revolution made available, few were more widespread than **novels and the penny press,** which included sales of millions of cheap books and magazines, especially in urban areas.

4.   The leading members of southern white society self-consciously built their world around the three pillars of **family, church, and neighborhood.**

    a.   The individualism common to northern culture proved less important to the value system of the South than did southern honor and the kinship of **southern families.**

    b.   **Southern entertainment,** which included horse racing, hunting, fishing, and other outdoor activities, reflected the essentially rural character of the South, while violent amusements were popular in the towns.

    c.   As more southerners found religion a form of recreation as well as a source of spiritual nourishment, the **camp meeting** became more staid and respectable.

    d.   Southerners embraced **religious conservatism** together with a conviction that fundamental political and social subservience to God's will was vital to its culture.

    e.   In time, the union of plantation economic interests and Protestantism resulted in a distinctly **proslavery Christianity** in the South.

5.   Determined to shield themselves from their masters in some measure, slaves sought to achieve some distinct elements in their **private lives,** with or without their masters' consent.

    (Show Transparency 10-01: 1849 Handbill Offering $600 Reward for 3 Runaway Slaves)

    a.   The **slave family,** a vital element in the difficult rigor of slave life, emerged as a crucial, if rather unstable, institution separate from white oversight.

    b.   **White missions** to the slaves exhibited southern evangelical preachers' abandonment of their hostility toward slave religiosity and their strong desire to Christianize slaves as well as slaveholders.

    c.   **Slave Christians** ignored much of the teachings of the white missionaries who sought to use religion as a means of assuring slave submissiveness, developing instead their own blend of African-American Christianity.

    d.   Invariably, **religion and revolt** came together in the violent insurrections of Denmark Vesey in South Carolina and **Nat Turner** in Virginia.

    e.   **Rebellions** such as these forced Virginians and other southerners to reconsider the institution of slavery, as they finally recognized that their sense of security was an illusion.

Conclusion: In the wake of the changes that accompanied the market revolution, a distinct set of American cultural values emerged, although with distinct differences north and south of the Mason–Dixon Line. Adherence to republican values and a wholesale embrace of market capitalism characterized the new culture of the northern middle class, while southerners were more reticent about embracing market forces, choosing instead to continue to rely on their well-ensconced plantation economy. In truth, they simply could not conceive of an alternate system.

FOCUS ON FEATURES

American Album: P. T. Barnum's American Museum, p. 370
History Through Film: *Beloved*, p. 380
Link to the Past: *Africans in America* (PBS), p. 379

TEACHING RESOURCES

Harriet Beecher Stowe: Uncle Tom's Cabin offers an abridged version of the George Aiken dramatization. Films for the Humanities & Sciences (45 minutes, color).

The West, episode two, examines the early, yet steady expansion of Americans into the West. PBS Video (55 minutes).

Working for the Lord discusses the impact of religion on the lives of eighteenth- and nineteenth-century Americans. Republic Pictures Home Video (52 minutes).

Chapter 11

SOCIETY, CULTURE, AND POLITICS, 1820s–1840s

CHAPTER SUMMARY

By the 1840s, the Whig and Democratic parties had well-defined constituencies. In the North and West, Whigs drew the support of merchants, factory owners, native-born factory workers, artisans, and middle-class evangelists. Whigs pushed for government action to accelerate the market revolution and to promote a moral code that involved Sabbath observance, temperance, and Bible-based schools. In the South, Whigs shared their northern colleagues' support for economic development but shunned their program for government-backed moral reform.

Democrats received the backing of cultural traditionalists, both from the North and South: farmers from areas bypassed by the market revolution and religious groups ranging from Irish Catholics in the cities to Baptists, Methodists, and Disciples of Christ in the South. The latter groups supported individual moral reform but rejected government interference in moral matters.

In the politics of social reform, both parties agreed that government should support common schools. Differences arose, though, over control. Whigs sought state-level centralization of schools; Democrats called for self-control for each local school district. Whigs wanted a state-imposed uniform curriculum; Democrats wanted a cheaper, locally controlled alternative.

In the movement to reform criminals, Whigs pushed for prisons that emphasized rehabilitation. They felt that a prison's controlled setting would provide inmates with work and discipline and would turn them into good citizens. Most Democrats viewed rehabilitation with skepticism and wanted prisons to punish criminals for their antisocial behavior. The Auburn Prison system, a compromise between the two camps, became the legislature's favorite.

By the 1820s and 1830s, reform movements of a bewildering variety swept through the nation. With the founding of the American Society for the Promotion of Temperance in 1826, the most popular reform of the era emerged. To assault the nation's alcohol problem, local, state, and national temperance organizations formed. Temperance, abstinence, and, finally, state-imposed prohibition drew reformers' support. With the formation of the Washingtonian Society in 1840, reformed drunkards contributed to the movement as well.

Race relations changed dramatically in the same era. While most whites in America remained committed to racial superiority over blacks, a minority of northern whites eventually embraced abolition. For free blacks in the North, life became even more uncertain as a new wave of European immigrants threatened their economic position and helped to create hostilities that led to race riots in Philadelphia and New York City. Democratic ideologues charged that blacks were not fit to be citizens in the white man's republic; Whigs offered lukewarm support for black citizenship.

Abolitionists from 1831 onward rejected the gradual emancipation and repatriation schemes of the American Colonization Society and demanded an immediate end to slavery and full civil and legal rights for blacks. Abolitionism thus became the most controversial reform of the era. Despite enormous opposition from both political parties, abolitionists brought the slavery question to the public arena and recast the debate over slavery into terms of political power and civil liberties.

Women, particularly those from a northern middle-class evangelical background, found a semblance of power in the reform movements. Using their newfound role as protector of family values, women launched a crusade to reform prostitutes and to curb male sexual excesses. Through their work in the abolition movement, many women began to perceive the need for women's rights legislation. Beginning around 1840, they lobbied state legislatures and achieved rights to own property, earn their own wages, and take custody of children in divorce cases. At the Seneca Falls convention in 1848, women activists began their quest for the right to vote.

LIBERTY, EQUALITY, POWER: A THEMATIC BRAID

Equality became a goal in the 1830s and 1840s for a significant portion of American women. This quest for equality grew in large measure from their experiences in the moral reform and abolitionist movements. Women rejected the concept of separate spheres for males and females, and they insisted that each individual, male or female, should be allowed to achieve his or her full potential. At their women's rights meetings, they began the pursuit of suffrage rights that would last several decades.

White men continued to seek power through development of economic and political opportunities. The Whig Party was the preference of those who enthusiastically embraced the market revolution. Whigs also pushed for the federal government to promote more internal improvements, banks, and schools, as well as moral restraint. For those who supported the new economic order but still held deep suspicions about excessive government involvement in the economy and in private life, the Democrats were the party of choice.

For free blacks in the North, political power and equality remained elusive. Their economic power even declined in these two decades as they faced economic competition from the Irish and other immigrants. Their social position declined, and anti-abolitionist sentiment and political demagoguery erupted in the form of race riots. For enslaved blacks, growing support for the abolitionist movement by whites and blacks alike meant that the morality of slavery was now in question to a degree never seen before in the nation. The abolitionists' promise of racial equality after the demise of slavery became a goal—and a dream—which all blacks could endorse.

For middle-class evangelists, liberty and equality before God could be pursued best through a many-faceted reform crusade. The millennium would arrive when Christian Americans, aided by their government, eliminated ignorance, alcohol, Sabbath-breaking, prostitution, sexual excesses, and other vices. Schools would form the character of the young, and prisons would reform the character of the criminal.

IDENTIFICATIONS

Democratic Party
Horace Mann
New York Herald
Auburn system
William Seward
Native American Party
Dorothea Dix
American Temperance Society
Washington Temperance Society
American Colonization Society
The Liberator
Fifteen-Gallon Law

Whig Party
American Anti-Slavery Society
Sojourner Truth
George Bancroft
Philadelphia system
Female Moral Reform Society
New York Magdalen Society
The Advocate of Moral Reform
Sarah Grimké
Women's Rights Convention
William Lloyd Garrison
Daniel Webster

CHRONOLOGY

1816	African Methodist Episcopal Church forms in Philadelphia.
	American Colonization Society created to send blacks to Africa.
1819	Prison reform system implemented at Auburn, New York.
1826	Reformers set up American Society for the Promotion of Temperance.
	Lyman Beecher publishes sermons against alcohol.
1830	Alexis de Tocqueville tours the United States.
1831	William Lloyd Garrison's *The Liberator* begins publication in Boston.
	New York Magdalen Society's report on prostitution shocks the city and launches the moral reform crusade.
1833	Abolitionists found the American Anti-Slavery Society.
1834	Anti-abolition mob riots in New York.
	First major race riot breaks out in Philadelphia.
1835	American Anti-Slavery Society commences postal campaign agitation.
1838	Massachusetts legislature passes Fifteen-Gallon Law.
1840	Washington Temperance Society forms as an organization for reformed drunkards.
1844	Native American Party wins New York City elections.
	First Women's Rights Convention held in Seneca Falls, New York.
1851	Maine becomes first state to enact statewide prohibition.
1860	New York State passes Married Women's Property Act.

THEMATIC TOPICS FOR ENRICHMENT

1. What issues united southern and northern Whigs? What issues divided them?
2. Discuss the banking situation in the United States after the destruction of the second Bank of the United States.
3. What were the differences between Whigs and Democrats in their plans for public education?
4. Why were Catholic parents upset with public schools and determined to establish church-controlled schools?
5. Discuss the differences between the Philadelphia system and the Auburn system for prison reform.
6. Which social reform of the era did the South support most enthusiastically? Why?
7. Describe the different ways that temperance reformers tried to curtail the consumption of alcohol.
8. What was the response of free blacks to declining economic, political, and social conditions in the 1830s and 1840s?
9. What caused the race riots of the 1830s in Philadelphia and New York?
10. How did abolitionists during this period differ from antislavery advocates that had come before them?
11. Describe the reform efforts of the Female Moral Reform Society.
12. How were abolitionism and the women's rights movement linked together?

GEOGRAPHY OBJECTIVES

1. What states comprised the Old Northwest (p. 298)?
2. On a map of North, Central, and South America, identify Haiti, Mexico, Peru, Chile, and Colombia (p. 36).
3. Find Liberia and its capital, Monrovia, on a map of Africa (p. 12).

SUGGESTED ESSAY TOPICS

1. Contrast the Whig and Democratic parties of the 1830s and 1840s. Who were their respective leaders and constituents, and what were their ideologies?
2. Compare the first party system of Federalists and Republicans with the second party system of Whigs and Democrats.
3. Define "social reform" and discuss its many goals in the 1830s and 1840s.
4. Explain the relationship between religion and politics in the second party system.
5. Characterize the life and struggles of free blacks in antebellum America.
6. Describe life in America during the first half of the 1800s, with regard to the following issues: population growth, health, immigration, and urbanization.

SUGGESTED WEB ACTIVITY FOR THE CLASSROOM

Ain't I a Woman?—Sojourner Truth

   http://www.discover.net/~dansyr/truth.html

This is the text of Sojourner Truth's famous speech delivered in 1851 at the Women's Convention in Akron, Ohio. It is still inspiring today.

LECTURE OUTLINE

1. As politics became more institutionalized, politicians had to compete for specific **constituencies,** largely based on region, class, and cultural values.
   a. **The North and West,** dominated by commercial farmers and enterprising immigrants, became the key locus of support for the emerging **Whig Party,** with Democratic minorities there coming mainly from the working class.
   b. Both parties had significant support in the South, with the **Democratic Party** popular among yeomen who owned few or no slaves and wanted little government interference, and the Whig Party dominated by plantation owners and their neighbors.
2. The **politics of economic development** were played out in the two-party rivalry of Democrats and Whigs, with the differences between the parties more a matter of method than of end result.
   a. No issue was more central to the parties than that of the nature of **government and its limits,** with the Whigs arguing that a forceful, benign government would benefit the entire society and Democrats insisting that citizens must have the power to control the central government's inevitable excesses.
   b. Like Jefferson's Republicans, Jackson's Democrats believed **banks** were of dubious morality, with the national bank especially evil.

© 2002 Thomson Learning, Inc.

c. The Whigs contended that **internal improvements** fostered economic growth, and therefore should be funded by the federal government, while Democrats voiced concerns about excessive debt and corruption.

3. Members of both major parties fought vociferously over **social reform,** especially as it became clear that reform issues influenced election results.

   a. Citizens in the North and West gave more support to **public schools** with state oversight, while southerners wanted to spend less money and maintain local control.

   b. As America's immigrants became more varied, **ethnicity and religion** took on a greater significance in **the schools.**

   c. State investment in **prisons** grew dramatically in the period, with New Jersey following the Pennsylvania system of solitary confinement and others following the "Auburn system," which relied on silence for discipline.

   d. Urged on by humanitarian reformers such as Dorothea Dix of Boston, states funded the construction of **asylums** to house the insane and care for them humanely.

   e. Cultural homogeneity and political conservatism inhibited the South from taking similar aggressive steps on **social reform** as had the North.

4. The **politics of alcohol** was so great an issue that often the temperance question constituted the major difference between Whigs and Democrats.

   a. The fight to prohibit **ardent spirits** became the obsession of many Americans, who started temperance organizations such as the American Temperance Society.

   (Show Transparency 11-01: Cartoon, "The Drunkard's Progress")

   b. The **origins of prohibition,** rooted in New England and exemplified by the short-lived "Fifteen-Gallon Law" of 1838, illustrated the societal divisions, with supporters of alcohol continuing to find ways to circumvent virtually every law.

   c. Citizens increasingly illustrated the **democratization of temperance** by willingly giving up drinking but opposing legislation designed to make the practice illegal; the Washington Temperance Society was the main public proponent of such views.

   d. Whig disapproval of the Washingtonians' tactics, especially their indulgence in popular culture activities, led to a series of **temperance schisms** in the 1840s.

   e. Ethnicity and alcohol became the focus of political and social discord by the 1850s, with the immigration of many **Irish and Germans** whose culture included drinking.

5. When it became clear that slavery was becoming more entrenched, the **politics of race** became increasingly contentious, threatening to divide the country along sectional and religious lines.

   a. Through the 1820s, **free blacks** in the North constituted a significant minority that participated in a wide variety of jobs.

   b. As growing numbers of immigrants displaced blacks from the work force, black leaders such as Frederick Douglass and Sojourner Truth emerged to fight both southern slavery and northern **discrimination.**

   c. While discrimination was widespread in antebellum America, **Democratic racism** especially encouraged a systematic attempt to equate American citizenship solely with being white.

   d. Antebellum America, especially Democratic ideologues, supported scientists who espoused a number of malignant **conceptions of racial difference.**

   e. The **beginnings of antislavery** feelings dated to years prior to the American Revolution, but most white antislavery advocates believed that the end of slavery would necessitate the removal of blacks from America; most blacks vehemently disagreed.

    f.   **Abolitionists** such as William Lloyd Garrison believed that slavery was a sin, and as such it had to be removed immediately, not gradually.

    g.   Copying other reformers, abolitionists began to use various active forms of **agitation** to raise whites' consciousness of their complicity in the institution of slavery.

6.   As with the issue of slavery, Whigs and Democrats differed on the **politics of gender and sex.**

    a.   Numerous reform groups sought to curb dangerous and licentious human **appetites,** such as overindulgence in food or sex.

    b.   **Moral reform,** through organizations such as the less than successful New York Magdalen Society, was proposed as a means to improve society through social rather than political avenues.

    c.   From the 1820s onward, middle-class women began to equate their subservient position with that of blacks, and their participation in the abolitionist movement culminated in the **Seneca Falls Convention of 1848.**

Conclusion: The society, culture, and politics of the decades of the 1820s, 1830s, and 1840s incorporated changing attitudes toward family, religion, race, class, ethnicity, and more. As the United States became an increasingly democratic, aggressive nation, America's cultural institutions adapted to serve the ideological needs of a people on the move, but Democratic white males fought to maintain their own position of power in both their families and their societies.

FOCUS ON FEATURES

American Album: The Bulwark of the Republic, p. 408
History Through Film: *Not for Ourselves Alone,* p. 414
Link to the Past: Papers of Elizabeth Cady Stanton and Susan B. Anthony (Model Editions Project), p. 412

TEACHING RESOURCES

"Harriet Tubman" and "Sojourner Truth" are video biographies in the twelve-part *The Black Americans of Achievement* video collection. Filmic Archives (30 minutes).

The Freedom Station is a drama about the Underground Railroad that is set in a "safe house" in 1850. It explores the concept of freedom versus the reality of being free. Filmic Archives (30 minutes).

Mr. Lincoln of Illinois re-creates the era and the man in this documentary about Lincoln during his prairie years. Films for the Humanities & Sciences (30 minutes, color).

Elizabeth Cady Stanton and Susan B. Anthony examines the lives of the women's rights pioneers. Films for the Humanities & Sciences (24 minutes, color).

Roots of Resistance details the story of the Underground Railroad in graphic, compelling terms. PBS Video (60 minutes).

Chapter 12

JACKSONIAN DEMOCRACY

CHAPTER SUMMARY

Jacksonian Democracy arose in great measure from reactions to the Missouri crisis of 1819 and the economic recession of the same year. In both the North and South, political leaders began to reconstruct the limited-government, states' rights coalition that had defined Jeffersonian republicanism. By 1828, this coalition would become the new Democratic Party.

When the Missouri crisis revealed the South's commitment to slavery and the North's growing resentment of the South's political power, political realignment began in earnest. The simultaneous collapse of the market economy further divided the political groups, as some now blamed the banks for the collapse. Others defended the banks and the economic structure they had fostered. Political realignment gained momentum with the election of 1824, when four presidential candidates emerged from the old Republican Party.

By 1828, Andrew Jackson's wing of the Republican Party was becoming the Democratic Party. Charging that the nation had gone astray because of selfishness, greed, and "corrupt bargains," Jackson called for a return to government by the Democratic majority. John Quincy Adams's version of republicanism, according to Jackson, called for excessive government spending, high taxes, government intrusion into private matters, and special privileges for the economic elite. The presidential campaign, filled with mudslinging propaganda from both camps, brought Jackson and his new party into power.

As an example of his states' rights commitment, Jackson allowed the southern states to declare sovereignty over Native American lands within their boundaries and pushed for removal of the tribes to the West. His commitment to nationalism, however, resulted in his clash with South Carolinians over nullification of the Tariff of 1828. In Jackson's mind, a state's right to nullify federal legislation was tantamount to disunion; disunion was not a right, but an act of treason.

In economic matters, Jacksonians championed the producing classes over the privileged elite, even making war on the second Bank of the United States on their behalf. To Jackson, the bank was a government-sponsored concentration of power and privilege. Jackson's opponents saw the bank as a stabilizing force and a necessary institution for economic expansion.

By 1834, Jackson's opponents had converted John Adams and Henry Clay's "national republicanism" into the Whig Party. Martin Van Buren and the Democrats continued the Jacksonian ascendancy in 1836, but in the 1840 campaign, William Henry Harrison and the Whigs became part of a national party that successfully challenged the Democrats and gained the presidency. The new two-party system that had been forming since 1819 was now complete.

LIBERTY, EQUALITY, POWER: A THEMATIC BRAID

How to acquire power—more than liberty and equality—was the question for the generation of the 1820s and 1830s. Beginning with the Missouri crisis, southern leaders saw any attempt to stop slavery's expansion as an attempt to limit southern political power. Northern leaders, indeed, viewed the expansion of the slave trade as the South's quest for even more political power.

In the view of Andrew Jackson and the Democratic Party, power had been lost to those who pushed for banks, paper money, and other financial complexities in the market economy. The second Bank of the United States was the worst usurpation of power yet. Also a great danger, the Jacksonians believed, was the growing power of the federal government, as it spent more money on internal improvements, raised taxes, and catered to the privileged. John Quincy Adams, Henry Clay, and their kind, Jacksonians charged, were betraying the republic to greed, corruption, and elitism.

For southern radicals such as John C. Calhoun, even the Democrats' support of states' rights was not enough to protect South Carolina from the federal government. Other sections of the nation, they feared, already had too much power that could affect the South's economic and political future. Only the right to nullify federal actions could save a state's liberty.

In the ongoing struggle for territory in Georgia and other southern states, Native Americans and whites sought the favor of the federal government. Native Americans wanted to retain sovereignty and asked merely that the federal government uphold its treaties; whites asked for sovereignty over all land within state boundaries and wanted tribal claims abolished.

For most Americans, equality still meant white equality. Jacksonians carried the issue into the political arena, charging that political or social systems differing from theirs challenged this equality.

IDENTIFICATIONS

Sacajawea

Sioux

Arkansas Territory

Force Bill

gag rule

Peggy Eaton

Nicholas Biddle

Specie Circular

Bank Veto Message

Pet Banks

American System

"Corrupt Bargain"

"Spoils System"

Adams–Onís Treaty

Worcester v. *Georgia*

(Five) Civilized Tribes

Tariff of 1828

Meriwether Lewis and William Clark

Missouri Compromise

Nat Turner

Panic of 1819

John Quincy Adams

second Bank of the United States

Era of Good Feelings

Martin Van Buren

William Crawford

Independent Treasury Bill

Panic of 1837

Whigs

"Tippecanoe and Tyler Too"

Log Cabin Campaign

Trail of Tears

Denmark Vesey conspiracy

nullification

CHRONOLOGY

1804–1806	Lewis and Clark expedition explores upper Louisiana and crosses the Continental Divide.
1816	Congress charters second Bank of the United States.
1819	Panic of 1819 marks first failure of the national market economy.
	Crisis arises over Missouri's admission to the Union.
	Adams–Onís Treaty extends American border to the Pacific Ocean.
1820	Missouri Compromise adopted.
	Maine becomes the twenty-third state.

1821	Missouri becomes the twenty-fourth state.
1822	Denmark Vesey conspiracy uncovered in South Carolina.
1823	Monroe Doctrine written by John Quincy Adams.
1824–1825	Adams wins presidency over Andrew Jackson.
	Adams appoints Henry Clay Secretary of State.
	Jacksonians charge "corrupt bargain" between Adams and Clay.
1827	Cherokees in Georgia declare themselves a republic.
1828	Jackson defeats Adams for presidency.
	"Tariff of Abominations" passed by Congress.
	John C. Calhoun's Exposition and Protest presents nullification doctrine.
1830	Congress passes Indian Removal Act.
	Marshall hands down verdict in case of *Cherokee Nation* v. *Georgia*.
1831	Nat Turner's rebellion extinguished in Virginia.
1832	"Bank War" erupts in Washington politics.
	Jackson reelected over Henry Clay.
	Jackson vetoes bill to recharter the Bank of the United States.
1833	Force Bill and Tariff of 1833 end the nullification crisis.
1834	Whig Party formed.
1836	House of Representatives adopts "gag rule" to table abolitionists' petitions.
	Martin Van Buren elected president.
1837	A severe economic depression begins with the Panic.
1838	"Trail of Tears" begins as army conducts forced march of Cherokees to the Indian Territory.
1840	Whig William Henry Harrison defeats Van Buren for the presidency.
	Congress passes Independent Treasury Bill.

THEMATIC TOPICS FOR ENRICHMENT

1. How did the North and the South react to Missouri's petition to enter the Union?
2. Discuss the causes of the Panic of 1819. What role did banks play in this recession?
3. Who were the presidential candidates in 1824? What did each have to offer to the voters?
4. Discuss Andrew Jackson's background, character, and political philosophy.
5. How did John Quincy Adams differ from Jackson in regard to background and political philosophy?
6. Discuss the 1828 election in terms of the issues and the propaganda that each put forth.
7. Describe the Indian-removal issue from either the point of view of the Georgia government or from the point of view of the Cherokees.
8. Explain John C. Calhoun's nullification doctrine and explain why Andrew Jackson opposed it.
9. Describe the controversy surrounding Peggy Eaton, and explain how the situation contributed to political problems between Jackson and Calhoun.
10. Discuss the Bank War from the viewpoints of Andrew Jackson and Nicholas Biddle.

GEOGRAPHY OBJECTIVES

1. Divide the United States into approximate regions: New England, Chesapeake, Deep South, Middle States, Northwest, and Southwest (p. 425).

2. Plot the expedition of Lewis and Clark up the Missouri River. Identify the locations of the various Indian tribes mentioned in the chapter (p. 458).

3. Find on a map the Missouri Compromise line of 36 degrees, 30 minutes. Identify free and slave states (p. 456).

4. Sketch the United States' southern border after the Adams–Onís Treaty of 1819 (p. 450).

SUGGESTED ESSAY TOPICS

1. Compare and contrast Andrew Jackson's political career and his views on government with those of Thomas Jefferson. How would you compare the two men's attitudes about "the people"?

2. Explain the impact of the Missouri debates on the politics of the Jacksonian era. Why did Thomas Jefferson call the controversy "a fire-bell in the night"?

3. Define the term *nationalism*. In what ways is nationalism a positive characteristic for a people? In what ways is it a negative one?

4. Evaluate the presidency of Andrew Jackson in light of his early life and early political history. Give attention to each of the following: the spoils system, nullification, the Bank War, and Indian removal.

SUGGESTED WEB ACTIVITY FOR THE CLASSROOM

Cherokee Trail of Tears: Other Paths

http://www.tngenweb.org/cherokee_by_blood/trail.htm

This site provides information that has been gathered concerning several detachments of Georgia Cherokee allowed to travel the Trail semi-independently. It is a moving site, discussing possible "desertions," and presenting demographic information on births, deaths, etc.

LECTURE OUTLINE

1. The year **1819** was a volatile one in the United States as debates over Missouri statehood and the bank panic set the stage for tumultuous events in the subsequent two decades, including the formation of a new Democratic Party led by Andrew Jackson.

   a. The **West** from 1803 to the 1840s was a land of bold exploration, methodical settlement, Sioux domination of other Indian tribes, and eventually the inevitable debate over slavery.

   b. Congress was almost paralyzed by sectional arguments over **Missouri statehood** and the fate of slavery in the Louisiana Territory.

   c. Congress averted disaster with the passage of the **Missouri Compromise,** which made Missouri a slave state and Maine a free state and also established a northern boundary for the expansion of slavery in the Louisiana Purchase territory.

    d.   The **Panic of 1819** caused the collapse of many banks, brought economic depression to many parts of the nation, and fostered a growing resentment toward the National Bank.

2.   Events of 1819 and 1820 led to a **Republican revival** of Jacksonian ideals, with virtually every national political figure seeming to call for small government, sectional peace, and government noninterference in slavery.

    a.   New Yorker **Martin Van Buren** led the way toward the construction of a new, more modern Democratic Party.

    b.   The **election of 1824** proved a fiasco with none of the four candidates garnering an electoral majority, although Jackson led in both popular and electoral votes.

    c.   With no candidate receiving an electoral plurality, the decision was made in the House of Representatives. Speaker Henry Clay's support of John Quincy Adams and Adams's subsequent appointment to the post of Secretary of State led to wide-scale accusations that a **"corrupt bargain"** had been struck between Clay and Adams.

    d.   Between 1825 and the next election, a veritable **Jacksonian melodrama** ensued, in which Jackson's men publicly lamented their candidate's unfair exclusion from the nation's highest office.

3.   The nation found itself in the midst of the **rebirth of sectionalism** under the guise of two highly contentious personalities, Jackson and Adams.

    a.   The **Adams–Onís Treaty** and the promulgation of the **Monroe Doctrine** moved American nationalism to a much larger international arena.

    b.   Adams's ideas about **nationalism at home** and his educational and scientific initiatives failed to take root in a Congress that viewed him as an enemy of democracy.

    c.   The **strength of the Democratic Party** stemmed directly from the public persona of Andrew Jackson and the behind-the-scenes machinations of Martin Van Buren.

    d.   Jackson's victory in the **election of 1828** vindicated the general and demonstrated the power of Van Buren's emerging party machine.

    e.   Sympathetic contemporaries called Jackson's March 4, 1828, inauguration, a **people's inauguration,** while skeptics viewed it as a display of the debauchery of the common folk.

    f.   Contemporaries termed Jackson's open replacement of government appointees with his own political operatives the **spoils system,** while the president insisted he was merely firing incompetents who were taking advantage of their exalted positions.

4.   Elections from the 1820s to the Civil War demonstrate the crucial ties between **Jacksonian Democracy and the South,** even as differences arose in party ranks.

    a.   Simmering tensions between southerners and Indians, whose land claims proved anathema to expansionists, centered on Georgia's desire to dispossess the Cherokees.

    b.   Jackson's explicit approval of the official government policy known as **Indian Removal** led to his public disavowal of the Court's decision in the case of *Worcester v. Georgia.*

    c.   From Jefferson to Jackson, **Southern opposition to the tariff** continued unabated, especially after the hodgepodge Tariff of 1828 that benefited other regions while hurting the South.

    d.   In response to the artificially high tariff rates, South Carolinian John C. Calhoun championed the doctrine of state **nullification** of federal law.

    e.   The dispute over the reputation of Secretary Eaton's wife among the wives of Jackson's Cabinet resulted in the **"petticoat wars"** that split the Administration between her attackers and defenders.

    f.   The Eaton affair and the publication of the vice president's criticism of Jackson's actions during the Seminole War led to the **fall of Calhoun** as Jackson anointed Martin van Buren as his successor.

(Show Transparency 12-01: "Despotism" Cartoon)

    g.   The sectional dispute over slavery erupted around Congress's debate over abolitionists' **petitions,** its use of the **gag rule** to avoid the issue, and informal censorship of the southern mails to ban anti-slavery tracts.

5. **Jacksonian Democracy** feared the excessive control of **the market revolution,** even as supporters worked to reconcile themselves to finding ways to benefit from it.

    a.   Most businessmen supported the rechartering of the **second Bank of the United States,** but Jackson, along with many other Americans, viewed the Bank as a serious threat to the republic.

    b.   When the president vetoed the second Bank's rechartering bill, a **bank war** ensued as the "monster bank" became the central issue of the 1832 presidential campaign.

    c.   The **beginnings of the Whig Party** date from the bank war and Jackson's heavy-handed and highly personal style of governance; its members were, first and foremost, opposed to Jackson.

    d.   Jackson's supporters believed that a **balanced budget** would ensure that the government remained relatively small and unobtrusive, as well as less prone to corruption.

6. The birth of the Whigs and the consolidation of the Jacksonian Democrats brought about the **second American party system.**

    a.   Jackson's inflationary bank policies contributed to the Panic of 1837 and made the reelection of **"Martin Van Ruin"** in 1840 a virtual impossibility.

    b.   The patently crude political machinations of both Whigs and Democrats in the **election of 1840,** such as the dispensing of massive quantities of hard cider, were caricatured in the emerging popular press of the day.

    c.   Despite many shenanigans, the election of 1840 instituted several decades of high voter turnout and ensured the success of an American electoral system driven by **two parties.**

Conclusion: Despite Jacksonian support for minimal government, the economic growth, territorial expansion, and remarkable immigration of the 1830s and 1840s forced both political parties to actively pursue control of the national government to accomplish their highly political ends. Echoing the sentiments of the Jeffersonians and supported by a strong party machine, the Democratic Party proved far more adept at winning national office than did their Whig opponents.

FOCUS ON FEATURES

American Album: Log Cabins and Hard Cider, p. 432
History Through Film: *Amistad*, p. 446
Link to the Past: A Hypertext on American History: Presidents (United States Information Agency), p. 443

TEACHING RESOURCES

When the White Man Came briefly describes life among the major tribes across the United States at the time of European arrival. Films for the Humanities & Sciences (13 minutes, color).

The Trail of Tears focuses on white expansion and the impact on Native American cultures. Films for the Humanities & Sciences (13 minutes, color).

© 2002 Thomson Learning, Inc.

Journals of Lewis & Clark re-creates with live action scenes the journey along the Missouri River. Filmic Archives (60 minutes).

Gone West examines the myths and realities of nineteenth-century life on the frontier. BBC/Time-Life Video (52 minutes).

Andrew Jackson: A Man for the People is the best portrait of the American president, Indian fighter, and symbol for an age. Arts and Entertainment Video (50 minutes).

Chapter 13

Manifest Destiny: An Empire for Liberty —or Slavery?

Chapter Summary

The near doubling of the nation's size in the 1840s gave credence to the concept of Manifest Destiny. Many Americans believed that Providence's grand design was for the United States to occupy all of North America. Intertwined with this was the racist belief that Native Americans, Mexicans, and anyone else who might stand in the way of expansion should be expelled. However, the question of slavery's role in this grand design still remained unanswered.

By the 1840s, the Oregon Country drew expansionists' attention. Oregon's discovery by "mountain men" and missionaries created a land rush known as "Oregon fever." At the same time, the Oregon Country became a source of contention between the United States and Great Britain.

Elsewhere, the westward march brought the Mormons under Brigham Young's leadership to arid lands around the Great Salt Lake. In territory still claimed by Mexico, Mormons sought isolation and self-determination in order to prevent clashes with their non-Mormon neighbors, the problem that had plagued the group in the East.

As the decade continued, traders and would-be settlers moved into New Mexico and California, sparking expansionist interest in those lands. At the same time, Texans, independent since 1836, agitated for annexation to the United States. James Knox Polk and the Democrats' victory in the 1844 election seemed a clear mandate for occupation of all the coveted territories: Oregon, New Mexico, California, and Texas.

In his first two years in office, Polk welcomed Texas into the American fold, split the Oregon Country with Great Britain, and offered to buy California and the rest of the Southwest from Mexico. Failing in the latter effort, Polk found pretexts for war with Mexico to achieve by conquest what negotiations had failed to produce.

The Mexican War deeply divided the nation, in large part because it brought into sharp focus the question of slavery's expansion. Deeply distrustful northerners saw Texas's annexation and the Mexican conflict as a territorial "grab" by the slave-owning southerners. Those same southerners, such as John C. Calhoun, saw the Wilmot Proviso and the Free Soil stance as efforts to contain the South and to destroy its political power. Seeking a middle position, supporters of popular sovereignty, such as Lewis Cass and Stephen A. Douglas, tried to make the issue of slavery's expansion a matter of territorial policy and not one of national debate that threatened to split North from South.

California's acquisition from Mexico and the almost simultaneous discovery of gold there deepened the growing rift between the two sections. By the end of 1849, with Californians clamoring for statehood, with Texas bitterly disputing the boundary with New Mexico, with abolitionists trying to rid the nation's capital of slavery, and with proslavery supporters agitating for a harsher fugitive-slave law, the Union faced its greatest crisis to date. The Compromise of 1850 settled the question of slavery's expansion in California but left the matter undecided in other areas, including possible new territories in the Caribbean and Central America. Meanwhile, the Compromise's Fugitive Slave Act, an ill-disguised proslavery effort to force northerners to show more support for slavery, brought mob action against slave catchers and federal officials trying to enforce the law. The publication of *Uncle Tom's Cabin* and other regional protests seemed a rallying cry for northern whites who saw the slave trade as a threat to their own civil liberties.

LIBERTY, EQUALITY, POWER: A THEMATIC BRAID

For many white Americans in the 1840s, Manifest Destiny incorporated both liberty and power. Expansionists almost reflexively believed it their free right to occupy virtually all of North America. Regardless of whether it was their destiny to do so, Americans knew they had the power to acquire the territory they coveted. The Anglo-Saxon version of civilization—the only version blessed by Providence, expansionists believed—must replace those of Native Americans, Mexicans, and even of religious dissenters such as the Mormons. The Democratic Party defined progress as spreading American institutions over space, while the Whigs defined it as improving institutions over time.

As America acquired more territory, another question of power arose. In the lands obtained by annexation, treaty, or war, which settlement pattern would be used? Would the South's reliance on slavery spread to these new areas, or would the North's commitment to free labor prevail? With slave states and free states at odds over a number of issues, the political implications of slavery's expansion became enormously important. That so many Americans in both North and South viewed this issue as one that permitted little room for compromise, doomed to failure the Compromise of 1850 and also other attempts to create harmony within the Union.

For other American groups, liberty, equality, and power became enmeshed in the westward movement as well, and they suffered in consequence. Indians lost territory and freedom of movement, as well as their cultural center, as their lands came under federal control. Black Americans had much at stake in regard to slavery's possible expansion. For American women, reluctance—and futile resistance—on the part of many women to move to the frontiers brought the realization that, in marriage and the family, patriarchy still ruled. They had little choice but to follow their men to the new lands.

IDENTIFICATIONS

John Tyler

Manifest Destiny

Lewis Cass

Oregon Trail

Great American Desert

Antonio López de Santa Anna

Sam Houston

"Fifty-four Forty or Fight!"

Winfield Scott

Rio Grande

Battle of Buena Vista

Treaty of Guadalupe Hidalgo

Anthony Burns

Wilmot Proviso

Ostend Manifesto

Liberty Party

Santa Fe Trail

Oregon fever

Mormon migration

Conscience Whigs

Free Soil Party

Compromise of 1850

Daniel Webster

Stephen A. Douglas

John C. Frémont

Fugitive Slave Act of 1850

Uncle Tom's Cabin

Harriet Beecher Stowe

filibustering

William Walker

CHRONOLOGY

1836   Mexican army captures the Alamo.

Texans defeat the Mexican army at San Jacinto.

1840s	"Young America" movement defines the nation's Manifest Destiny.
1842–1843	"Oregon fever" impels thousands to move to the Oregon Country.
1844	Anti-Mormon mob kills Joseph Smith in Illinois.
	James K. Polk elected president.
1845	United States annexes Texas.
1846	Mexican War begins.
	American settlers led by John C. Frémont capture Sonoma, California.
	Wilmot Proviso causes great controversy over slavery's expansion.
1847	Brigham Young leads the Mormons west to the Great Basin.
	Mexico City falls to the United States Army.
1848	Treaty of Guadalupe Hidalgo ends the Mexican War.
	Popular sovereignty proposed by Lewis Cass.
	Free Soil Party forms.
	Gold discovered in California.
	Zachary Taylor wins the presidency.
1849	California seeks admission as state.
1850	Henry Clay and Stephen A. Douglas craft the Compromise.
	John C. Calhoun and Zachary Taylor die.
	Millard Fillmore sworn in as president.
	California admitted as a free state.
1851	Fugitive slaves laws cause conflict in North.
1852	Harriet Beecher Stowe publishes *Uncle Tom's Cabin*.
1854	Ostend Manifesto issued.
	William Walker leads filibustering expedition to Nicaragua.

THEMATIC TOPICS FOR ENRICHMENT

1. Describe what Manifest Destiny meant for white laborers and farmers in the 1840s. What did it mean for slave owners?

2. Discuss what Manifest Destiny held in store for western Native Americans. What did Manifest Destiny mean for black Americans?

3. Discuss the various reasons Americans went west in the 1840s.

4. Why did Texans seek independence from Mexico in the 1830s? Why did they want the United States to annex Texas?

5. Discuss how events in California and the actions of President Taylor led to a sectional crisis at the end of 1849.

6. What were the provisions of the Fugitive Slave Act that upset northerners? Describe how northerners reacted to the act's enforcement.

GEOGRAPHY OBJECTIVES

1. On a map of the United States, identify the states carved out of Jefferson's Louisiana Purchase between 1803 and 1846 (p. 456).

2. Sketch the route of the Santa Fe Trail from Independence, Missouri, to Santa Fe, and the Oregon Trail from Independence to Portland, Oregon (p. 458).

3. Find the Oregon Territory on a map and contrast Polk's campaign pledge of 54°40′ with the ultimate treaty line of the forty-ninth parallel (p. 463).

4. On a map of the western United States, shade the territory acquired by the United States between the 1819 Adams–Onís Treaty and the Treaty of Guadalupe Hidalgo thirty years later (p. 467).

SUGGESTED ESSAY TOPICS

1. Define the concept of Manifest Destiny and assess its impact upon American politics in the 1840s.

2. Assess the causes and consequences of the United States' war with Mexico. Why did many Americans oppose the war?

3. Compare and contrast the platforms of the Liberty Party, the Free Soil Party, and the Conscience Whigs. What views did all three share?

4. What issues did the Compromise of 1850 resolve? Which ones did it not?

5. Describe the expansionism that took place in the United States during the first half of the 1800s, especially with regard to Texas, Oregon, and the Mexican War.

SUGGESTED WEB ACTIVITY FOR THE CLASSROOM

Museum of the City of San Francisco

  http://www.sfmuseum.org/hist2/gold.html

The museum has compiled a worthwhile site. One of the most interesting sections contains fourteen lithographic prints from the Gold Rush era, 1850–1857. These are presented in a timed Power Point presentation. The site contains many other items, some of which take some time to load. The prints load easily, however, and they would be good discussion starters.

LECTURE OUTLINE

1. Citizens of almost all regions of the country in the 1840s instinctively viewed **territorial growth** as the American way—as the country's God-given right; Indians on the frontier could not stop this onslaught.

    a. Many northerners understood that **Manifest Destiny** and slavery were intimately tied together, as new lands in the South experienced the expansion of the "peculiar institution."

    (Show Transparency 13-02: Map, Free and Slave States and Territories, 1848)

    b. Forged by the first seventeenth-century settlers, Americans' **westering impulse** in the 1800s proved as much a northern as a southern phenomenon.

    c. The **Oregon and California Trails** served as routes for literally hundreds of thousands to make their way, often at great peril, into the alluring lands of the West as "Oregon fever" swept the country.

    (Show Transparency 13-03: Map, Overland Trails, 1846)

    d. Joseph Smith gave his life in leading the remarkable **Mormon migration,** which culminated in Brigham Young's settlement of the Utah Territory in 1847.

e.   American expansionists, led by Sam Houston, declared their independence from Mexico and founded the **Republic of Texas** in March of 1836.

f.   Texans' desire to join the United States precipitated the **Annexation Controversy** in Congress during the administration of **John Tyler.**

g.   Dark horse candidate **James Knox Polk** made the acquisition of Texas and Oregon the key planks of his successful campaign for the presidency in 1844.

(Show Transparency 13-01: Anti-Polk Cartoon, 1846)

2.   Deliberate American provocations resulted in a two-year **war with Mexico;** in truth, the conflict was a land grab aimed at California and New Mexico.

(Show Transparency 13-04: Map, Principal Campaigns of the Mexican War, 1846–1847)

a.   The military campaigns of 1846 proved highly successful, particularly in California, but created a formidable Whig presidential prospect in **Zachary Taylor,** "Old Rough and Ready," who led his forces to successive victories in Texas.

b.   The military campaigns of 1847 proved even more successful, with the rather meager army of **Winfield Scott** ("Old Fuss and Feathers") performing an amphibious landing at **Vera Cruz,** decimating a larger Mexican force and capturing Mexico City.

c.   Northerners, ever skeptical of southern motives, publicly and vociferously expressed their heartfelt **antiwar sentiment.**

d.   Reservations about war aims led the House to pass the **Wilmot Proviso,** which sought the exclusion of slavery from all territory acquired in the war.

3.   The overlapping issues of territorial expansion and slavery dominated the politics of the **election of 1848** and promised to plague the short-lived presidency of Louisiana's Zachary Taylor.

a.   Northern antislavery activists founded the **Free Soil Party** upon the same principles as those of the Wilmot Proviso, and they sent eleven of their members to Congress.

b.   The year 1849 marked the start of the **gold rush** and the subsequent movement for **California statehood,** once again raising the issue of slavery.

4.   While hailed by many as the savior of the Union, the **Compromise of 1850** in its final form only delayed the ultimate breakdown of the party system.

a.   The **Senate debates** over the 1850 Compromise revolved around the efforts of Clay and Webster, who supported compromise, and Calhoun, who opposed it.

b.   The **passage of the Compromise** as an omnibus bill proved impossible but succeeded under the clever manipulation of freshman Senator Stephen A. Douglas of Illinois.

c.   Northerners found the **Fugitive Slave Law** abominable, especially after witnessing the shocking actions of slave catchers in their own streets.

d.   Southern representatives condemned **fugitive slave escapes,** such as that of Anthony Burns, while many antislavery advocates materially supported the Underground Railroad.

e.   No one event contributed more to antislavery sentiment than Harriet Beecher Stowe's *Uncle Tom's Cabin*, published in 1852 and reprinted many times subsequently.

5.   Southern expansionists sought through **filibustering** expeditions to acquire more lands for the expansion of slavery.

a.   Filibusterers, like the supporters of the Ostend Manifesto, believed that Manifest Destiny included American slave colonies in the Caribbean and Central America, as well as Cuba and Nicaragua.

b. The most remarkable of the *filibusteros* was William Walker, the **gray-eyed man of destiny** who, after naming himself president of Nicaragua, was later executed by a firing squad in Honduras while attempting another coup.

Conclusion: Americans termed "Manifest Destiny" the notion that North America ought to be the sole domain of white Americans and their institutions. Manifest Destiny justified the acquisition through war and treachery of over 1.1 million square miles of territory at the end of the 1840s. While few disavowed the acquisition of new territory, many northerners suspected that expansion westward was a vehicle for the expansion of the South's peculiar institution. Though the Compromise of 1850 seemed to have settled the issue, slavery would precipitate another crisis in Kansas a mere four years later.

FOCUS ON FEATURES

American Album: The California Gold Rush, p. 472
History Through Film: *The Alamo*, p. 460
Link to the Past: The Mexican War, p. 464

TEACHING RESOURCES

Frederick Douglass: When the Lion Wrote History is a documentary on the "most influential black man" of the nineteenth century. PBS Video (90 minutes).

The Donner Party gives the tragic history of the ill-fated group trying to reach California in 1846. PBS Video (90 minutes).

The Oregon Trail is a four-part documentary of the 1840s land rush to Oregon. Films for the Humanities & Sciences (25 minutes each, color).

"The Golden Land," in *The West of the Imagination* series, documents the West in the 1830s and 1840s. Films for the Humanities & Sciences (52 minutes, color).

Texas and the Mexican Cession profiles the history of Texas's quest for independence. Filmic Archives (14 minutes).

Gold Rush and the Settlement of California provides an account of the developments in 1848–1849 in the West. Filmic Archives (16 minutes).

The West, episodes two and three, discusses the American westward expansion often called Manifest Destiny. PBS Video (60 minutes each).

Chapter 14

THE GATHERING TEMPEST, 1853–1860

CHAPTER SUMMARY

Less than five years after the Compromise of 1850 had forged a fragile peace between the North and the South, the two sections found that peace shattered. Controversy over the Fugitive Slave Act and the reaction to *Uncle Tom's Cabin* contributed to the collapse of sectional harmony. Other factors included the demise of the Whig Party and the reemergence of the issue of slavery's expansion, particularly in the Kansas Territory.

Northern and southern Whigs had divided over the California question and what southern Whigs saw as Zachary Taylor's betrayal. By 1852, many had joined the southern Democrats and helped to elect that party's presidential candidate, Franklin Pierce. Further dividing the party was a new wave of nativism that drew many Whigs into the American Party—better known as the Know-Nothings. That party focused on anti-Catholic and anti-immigrant issues rather than those on which the Whig Party had been founded.

The Kansas–Nebraska Act destroyed the minimal peace that had been gained through the Compromise of 1850. Stephen A. Douglas's collaboration with David Atchinson and other proslavery leaders to organize the two territories on the basis of popular sovereignty—with the tacit understanding that Kansas would develop as a slave territory—infuriated northerners and reawakened fears of the "Slave Power" of the South. As a result of northern anger over the act's passage, northern Democrats lost much support, and the Republican Party emerged to replace the Whigs in a new two-party system. By 1856, the Republicans had constructed a strictly sectional but already powerful organization that was dedicated to wresting national power from the Democrats and preventing the spread of slavery to any new territory.

The settlement of Kansas in 1854 and 1855 proved that popular sovereignty was unworkable. Free-soil elements battled proslavery settlers, the latter aided by "border ruffians" from neighboring Missouri. By 1856, Kansas had both a proslavery territorial government and a free-soil government, with each claiming to be legitimate. When proslavery forces sacked the town of Lawrence and John Brown attacked Pottawatomie Creek, America began to refer to the area as "Bleeding Kansas."

The issue of Kansas divided the Democratic Party along sectional lines. President James Buchanan's ill-advised support of the territory's proslavery faction and its Lecompton Constitution forced Stephen Douglas to admit that the proslavery side (through election fraud and intimidation) had made a mockery of popular sovereignty. Douglas's insistence that fair elections be held in Kansas cost him southern Democratic support and virtually doomed his presidential hopes.

The sectional division deepened with the Dred Scott Supreme Court decision and the Panic of 1857. In the Scott case, the southern-dominated Court blasted both the free-soil and popular-sovereignty positions on slavery's expansion—only to discover that such an emotional issue as slavery's future in the territories could not be settled by a court ruling. Because the economic recession of 1857 seemed to affect the North more than the South, southern leaders could not resist touting their own slave-based economy as being superior to that of the free labor system in the North. According to George Fitzhugh and other southern apologists, the slave was better off and happier than the free worker in the North. Despite enormous northern economic expansion in the 1850s, James Hammond and other southern leaders proclaimed that "cotton is king."

The decade ended with violent reaction to John Brown's raid on Harper's Ferry. Brown's plans for a slave revolt reawakened the increasingly paranoid southerners' greatest fear. They perceived the North as containing many "John Browns" ready to launch further bloody attacks on the South. Even more ominous for the Union, they viewed the Republican Party as the harborer and instigator of fanatics such as Brown and vowed to leave the Union if Republicans won the presidency in 1860.

LIBERTY, EQUALITY, POWER: A THEMATIC BRAID

In the 1850s, Kansas became the prize in the quest by both the North and the South for more political power. More votes in Congress meant more control over the national agenda and the nation's future. Even more important for the proslavery side, the possibility that Kansas could become a slave territory meant that the northern blockade on slavery's expansion might end. Some southern leaders, such as David Atchinson, perceived Kansas as the first of many territories where slavery could be established successfully. So important was Kansas to the free-soil and proslavery camps that hundreds of families moved to Kansas to cast ballots for their particular stand on the slavery issue, and both sides were prepared to resort to violence if balloting failed to produce the desired results. More determined yet were proslavery Missourians who used force to win Kansas for their side.

The issue of the expansion of slavery involved such a struggle for power that traditional ways of settling such disputes—the ballot and the courts—worked less and less well as the decade progressed. Neither side accepted the outcome of the Kansas elections. Southerners threatened to leave the Union if voters ever put Republicans into power in the national government. After ruling on the Dred Scott case, the Supreme Court found that much of the nation cared little about what the courts had to say concerning slavery's expansion.

Meanwhile, definitions of liberty and equality were much debated. As Abraham Lincoln asked, were all men created equal, or did this truth apply only to white men? Did it apply to Protestants and not Catholics? Or did equality apply just to native-born citizens and not immigrants? Ultimately, the question became whether the United States was the champion of democracy for the master race only, or the champion of a political system that embraced whites and the other races, native-born and immigrant, men and women, Protestant and Catholic.

The depth of the sectional division over freedom was revealed when John C. Calhoun and other southerners proclaimed they were protecting the freedom of all whites by uniting all classes of whites to ensure that slavery of the black race continued. For Lincoln and many of his northern contemporaries, this could not be more wrong. Either slavery or freedom would have to die.

IDENTIFICATIONS

David R. Atchinson

Abraham Lincoln

McCormick Reaper

Kansas–Nebraska Act

Republican Party

King Cotton

Know-Nothings

nativism

Bleeding Kansas

Lecompton Constitution

Charles Sumner

"Crime against Kansas" Speech

Roger B. Taney

Freeport Question

Harper's Ferry

James Buchanan

Stephen A. Douglas

American System of Manufactures

DeBow's Review

John C. Frémont

The Impending Crisis of the South

Hinton Rowan Helper

Panic of 1857

Wendell Phillips

"border ruffians"

George Fitzhugh

Preston Brooks

Dred Scott

Lincoln–Douglas debates

John Brown

Pottawatomie Creek

ideology

CHRONOLOGY

1846	*DeBow's Review* first published in New Orleans.
1851	Crystal Palace exhibit in London draws great attention.
1852	The American (Know-Nothing) Party becomes significant political factor.
1854	Congress passes the Kansas–Nebraska Act.
	Republican Party forms in Wisconsin.
	"Know-Nothings" gain strength on nativist agenda.
1854–1856	Crimean War rocks Europe.
1855–1856	"Bleeding Kansas" develops.
1856	Lawrence, Kansas, sacked by proslavery mob.
	John Brown murders proslavery defenders at Pottawatomie Creek.
	Brooks canes Sumner in Senate chamber.
	James Buchanan wins presidency.
1857	Dred Scott decision issued by Supreme Court.
	Economic panic and recession.
	George Fitzhugh publishes *Cannibals All.*
	Hinton R. Helper issues *The Impending Crisis of the South.*
	Lecompton Constitution written by Kansas proslavery forces.
1858	Lincoln delivers his "House Divided" speech.
	Lincoln–Douglas debates.
1859	John Brown hanged after raid at Harper's Ferry.

THEMATIC TOPICS FOR ENRICHMENT

1. Discuss the motivations in 1854 for repealing the Missouri Compromise and organizing Kansas and Nebraska on the basis of popular sovereignty.
2. What was the "black belt," and why was it so named?
3. Why did "nativism" reemerge in the 1850s in the form of the "Know-Nothing" political movement? Who were the nativists' targets? Why?
4. Why did Kansas become "Bleeding Kansas" in the mid-1850s? Explain why Missourians believed that they had to interfere in Kansas' politics.
5. Discuss the issues behind the Dred Scott decision. Why did the Court rule the way it did? Why did many ignore its ruling?
6. Explain why the national economy expanded so greatly in the 1850s and how this expansion played a role in sectional politics.
7. Contrast George Fitzhugh's concept of slavery with that of Hinton R. Helper.
8. Compare the northern reaction to John Brown in 1859 with the southern reaction.
9. What were the differences between "free-labor ideology" and the southern version of *herrenvolk* democracy?

GEOGRAPHY OBJECTIVES

1. Locate Kansas and Nebraska on a map. Which states border Kansas (p. 494)?
2. Compare the transportation systems of the North and South in the 1850s (p. 500).
3. Outline the region named the "black belt," and identify which states it lies within (p. 506).

SUGGESTED ESSAY TOPICS

1. What was Stephen Douglas's rationale for the 1854 Kansas–Nebraska Act? Why did the passage of the act lead to "Bleeding Kansas" and so much discord in American politics?
2. What was the "free labor" ideology of the Republican Party?
3. Explain the Dred Scott case, Taney's decision, and their impact on sectional strife.
4. Compare and contrast the economies of the North and South in the 1850s. Why had they diverged so greatly in the preceding three decades?

SUGGESTED WEB ACTIVITY FOR THE CLASSROOM

Secession Era Editorials Project
"The Caning of Sumner (May 1856)"

 http://history.furman.edu/~benson/docs/sumenu.htm

Over sixty editorials from American newspapers are reprinted here, all concerning the Senate chamber incident that so polarized the country in the summer of 1856. This happening, already of great interest to students, can be even more effectively brought to life through the viewing and discussion of some of these editorials.

LECTURE OUTLINE

1. Nothing contributed more to the sense of sectional crisis than the fight over slavery in **Kansas.** The rise of the **Republican Party** in opposition to the spread of slavery, and to slaveholders' interests anywhere, guaranteed that slavery would dominate political debates for the remainder of the 1850s.

    a. The brainchild of Stephan A. Douglas of Illinois, the **Kansas–Nebraska Act** of 1854 repealed the Missouri Compromise line that had marked the northern border of slave expansion in the Louisiana Purchase.

    b. The sectional fighting over slavery and related issues led directly to the **death of the Whig Party,** as northern Whigs joined the new Republican Party.

2. Concerns over **immigration** and **nativism** proved important political issues that in other times might have overshadowed the growing crisis over slavery.

    a. A visceral fear among many Protestants of **immigrants in politics,** especially Catholics, resulted in the formation of the American, or Know-Nothing, Party.

    b. The rise of the **"Know-Nothings"** peaked with the unsuccessful candidacy of ex-president Millard Fillmore for president in 1856, on a platform of immigrant restriction and delay of full political rights to newcomers.

    c. The furor over slavery increased with the **decline of nativism,** itself crucial to any chance of Republican success in national politics.

3. A virtual civil war known as **Bleeding Kansas** broke out in that territory, as competing pro- and antislavery factions battled for supremacy and the right to control the legislature.

(Show Transparency 14-02: Map, Kansas–Nebraska and the Slavery Issue)

   a. Charles Sumner's **"Crime against Kansas"** speech so inflamed South Carolina Representative Preston Brooks that he nearly beat Sumner to death. Brooks' caning of the Massachusetts senator was as hailed in the South as it was condemned in the North.

   b. In Kansas, abolitionist John Brown carried out a vicious raid on proslavery settlers that left five people dead and the country in shock.

(Show Transparency 14-01: Congressman Preston Brooks beating Senator Charles Sumner, 1856)

4. The Republicans' first presidential candidate, John C. Frémont, ran well in the **election of 1856.** Though he failed to win enough border states to defeat Democrat James Buchanan, the growing strength of the Republican Party caused southerners once again to speak of secession.

   a. In the **Dred Scott case,** Supreme Court Chief Justice Roger B. Taney ruled that the Missouri Compromise constituted an illegal denial of the property rights of slaveholders and that slaves were not citizens and, therefore, could not sue in court.

   b. President Buchanan endorsed Kansas's blatantly proslavery Lecompton Constitution, despite the vehement opposition of Stephen Douglas and other northern Democrats.

5. The **economy in the 1850s** hummed along as economic production even outstripped the prodigious rate of population increase, and the United States surpassed every country except Great Britain.

(Show Transparency 14-03: Map, Main Transportation Routes in the 1850s)

   a. Contemporaries heaped praise on "Yankee ingenuity" and the so-called **"American system of manufactures,"** which incorporated the wide-scale use of interchangeable parts and other technical innovations.

   b. The **southern economy** grew rapidly in the 1850s, largely on the basis of growing worldwide demand for cotton.

   c. The inherent dangers of the **sovereignty of king cotton** were noted by James D. B. De Bow and other southerners who favored diversification and modernization of techniques.

(Show Transparency 14-04: Map, Slavery and Staple Crops in the South, 1860)

   d. While northern leaders espoused the glories of free labor, **labor conditions in the North** were often miserable, as wages were low and urban life unhealthy in the extreme. Overall, though, opportunities were greater in the North than anywhere else in the world.

   e. While the **Panic of 1857** hit hardest in the industrial areas of the North, the economic depression was short-lived even there.

   f. **Sectionalism and the Panic** went hand in hand, and northerners, though rescued in part by southern cotton sales, felt a growing resentment toward southern politicians' intransigence on economic reform measures.

   g. The **free labor ideology** of "free soil, free labor, free men" was at the heart of the Republican Party's sectional message in the 1850s.

   h. Republicans skillfully exploited the publication of North Carolinian Hinton Rowan Helper's *The Impending Crisis* to demonstrate how slavery negatively affected the material conditions of non-slaveholders.

   i. While few **southern non-slaveholders** seemed to be aware of the negative impact of slavery on their economic fortunes, most understood that their white skin made them part of the "ruling race" of their region.

© 2002 Thomson Learning, Inc.

6. The **Lincoln–Douglas debates** of 1858 served to highlight the deep divide over the morality of slavery in Illinois, and the North in general, and they quickly came to be regarded as perhaps the finest example of stump speech eloquence from the era.

   a. Abraham Lincoln stirred great controversy when, upon launching his bid for the Senate nomination, he declared that the Union could not forever remain "a house divided."

   b. Douglas lost any chance of southern extremist support for his 1860 presidential campaign when he espoused in his **"Freeport doctrine"** that citizens could effectively exclude slavery from the territories.

7. The capture of abolitionist **John Brown at Harper's Ferry** and his subsequent execution stirred the conscience of northerners who previously had considered abolitionists to be nothing less than dangerous disunionists.

Conclusion: Despite the efforts of many politicians, who feared for the Union, the myriad unsettling events of the 1850s reinforced the growing schism between slavery and freedom. The birth of the Republican Party and John Brown's raid at Harper's Ferry proved true the South's greatest fears, while the upcoming presidential election of 1860 would lead southerners to reconsider the value of remaining within the United States.

FOCUS ON FEATURES

American Album: The Lincoln–Douglas Debates, p. 512
History Through Film: *Abe Lincoln in Illinois*, p. 486
Link to the Past: The 1850s: An Increasingly Divided Union, p. 492

TEACHING RESOURCES

America Grows Up (1850–1900s) offers an overview of the nation's economic development. Filmic Archives (53 minutes).

On a Clear Day You Can See Boston describes the Irish immigration to the nation in the 1850s. Films for the Humanities & Sciences (52 minutes, color).

Go West, Young Man covers the Norwegian movement to the Midwest. Films for the Humanities & Sciences (52 minutes, color).

Out of Ireland focuses on Irish immigrants who arrived in the mid-nineteenth century. PBS Video (111 minutes).

Lincoln: Making of a President describes his formative years and his rise to national prominence during the Lincoln–Douglas debates. Movies Unlimited (60 minutes).

The Civil War: Union at Risk presents the prewar differences between North and South and emphasizes constitutional interpretation. Filmic Archives (25 minutes, color).

Chapter 15

SECESSION AND CIVIL WAR, 1860–1862

CHAPTER SUMMARY

The 1860 election completed the split between the North and the South. Unable to decide between popular sovereignty and proslavery platforms, the Democratic Party split into northern and southern fragments, ending the South's last political tie to the North. Southern Democrats chose John C. Breckinridge as their presidential candidate; northern Democrats picked Stephen A. Douglas. The Constitutional Union Party, mainly a collection of border-state former Whigs, opted to run Tennessean John Bell for the presidency. The Republicans, needing only to unite the North for victory, nominated Abraham Lincoln. After a lively campaign in which the Republicans broadened their appeal by adding economic issues to their platform and the southern Democrats vowed to leave the Union if they lost the election, the upstart Republican Party, just six years old, won virtually every northern state and with them the presidency.

Secession fever ran rampant in the South. Believing that secession was a constitutional right—simply the reverse of the decision to join the Union—South Carolina and six other Deep South states "withdrew" from the United States by February of 1861. Northerners argued that the decision to join the Union was irreversible, that the "doctrine of secession is anarchy." They bitterly opposed southerners on this constitutional issue. Efforts to reach a compromise in this national crisis, however, failed. Only the Crittenden proposal to guarantee slavery and to extend it into the territories drew much interest, and both Republicans and secessionists eventually rejected that idea.

In early February in Montgomery, Alabama, delegates from the seceded states created the Confederate States of America and called for the other eight slave states to join their new nation. For their constitution, they simply copied, word for word, much of the U.S. Constitution, changing it, primarily, only to give more power to the states and additional explicit protection to slavery. With the exception of a few military installations, such as Fort Sumter and Fort Pickens, the Confederates seized federal property and expelled U.S. officials from Confederate soil.

Lincoln's hopes to buy time to allow southern unionism to reassert itself collapsed with the Fort Sumter situation. Offering only humanitarian assistance to the fort's soldiers, the new president brilliantly turned Fort Sumter into a Confederate dilemma. In the predawn hours of April 12, the Confederates attacked the fort; thirty hours later Fort Sumter capitulated. With the Civil War underway, Lincoln asked the states for 75,000 volunteers to put down the rebellion.

For the border states especially, the time to choose sides had arrived. Virginia, North Carolina, Arkansas, and Tennessee went with the Confederacy. Missouri, Kentucky, Maryland, and Delaware chose to stay in the Union. In many of the border states, strong dissent on the secession issue resulted in isolated incidents of guerrilla warfare, creating wars within the Civil War.

The Union had enormous advantages over the Confederacy. In manpower, industrial output, banking resources, trade, and transportation, the North stood supreme over the South. But for a decisive victory, Union forces would have to conquer and occupy much of the South, whereas Confederate forces only needed to stop the northern invasions and bide their time until the northerners grew tired of war and went home.

Neither side believed that the war would last very long or had any idea of just how bloody the conflict would be. The rifle, with its "Minié ball" bullets, took a terrible toll on both sides and forced changes in tactics. Steam-powered, armor-plated naval ships, naval mines, and other innovations changed warfare on the seas. Railroads and telegraphs forced generals to adopt new strategies to match these technological advances.

Financing the war brought runaway inflation and economic misery to the South. Unable or unwilling to tax or borrow enough money, the Confederate government issued paper money, which rapidly became worthless. Also a failure was the South's King Cotton policy, which denied the Confederacy money from the production of cotton, its chief asset, and still did not force Great Britain and other European nations to give the Confederacy diplomatic recognition. The Union navy's blockade of southern shipping became more effective after 1862, and, with internal transportation problems within the Confederacy, food shortages afflicted a growing number of Confederate citizens.

Bull Run, the first major battle of the Civil War, elated southerners and stunned northerners as it turned into a Union debacle. Even after George McClellan regrouped northern forces and turned them into the formidable Army of the Potomac, Union fortunes in the Virginia theater did not improve greatly. McClellan's 1862 "peninsular campaign" failed to take Richmond, the Confederate capital. John Pope and his Union army failed to stop Robert E. Lee and his Army of Northern Virginia at the Second Battle of Bull Run and left Maryland open to Lee's invasion.

West of the Appalachians, the Union fared better. In February 1862, Ulysses S. Grant's forces took control of the Tennessee and Cumberland rivers by taking Forts Henry and Donelson. Nashville became the first Confederate state capital to fall to Union forces. After a setback on the first day of the Battle of Shiloh, Grant regrouped, won the battle, and forced the Confederates into northern Mississippi. Meanwhile, Union ships under David Farragut's command took control of the mouth of the Mississippi and forced New Orleans to capitulate. By the summer of 1862, the Confederacy controlled only Port Hudson and Vicksburg on the Mississippi.

LIBERTY, EQUALITY, POWER: A THEMATIC BRAID

The power struggle between North and South evolved from a political one in 1860 to a military one in 1861. Determined to force northern Democrats into supporting slavery's expansion by threatening to destroy the party, Deep South delegates at the 1860 national conventions bolted, snapping the Democratic tie between the two sections. Facing two Democratic presidential candidates and one from the Constitutional Union Party, Republicans were able to gain power merely by uniting the North. The Democratic split swept Lincoln into the presidency, and northern strength in Congress increased.

For southern leaders, this was an unacceptable shift in political fortunes. Since 1789, the president, the House Speaker, and the president pro tem of the Senate had been southerners two thirds of the time. The Supreme Court, too, had been a southern power base. Feeling their enormous influence on the nation's future direction slipping away, many southerners feared that the "southern way" had been so well contained by the Republican surge that they faced an uncertain future even within the South. The question for many southerners after Lincoln's victory was whether it was wise to stay in a Union that no longer protected southern interests or to secede and create their own union of slave states.

Did they have the right to secede? Southerners argued that secession was an option because states still retained their sovereignty after they had joined the Union. They now wished to reclaim this power to control their own affairs. Northerners vehemently disagreed. The Union was not a collection of sovereign states but an indivisible political entity. If one minority left the majority, other minorities would follow until the Union would be, as James Buchanan put it, a "rope of sand." As the war soon proved, secession was not a right, but a question of power—military power.

IDENTIFICATIONS

John C. Breckinridge

fire-eaters

Constitutional Union Party

Crittenden Compromise

Confederate States of America

Jefferson Davis

Fort Sumter

Major Robert Anderson

David Farragut

Army of the Potomac

Forts Henry and Donelson

Battle of Shiloh

Minié ball

Vicksburg

King Cotton diplomacy

greenbacks

blockade runners

Trent affair

The *Monitor* and the *Virginia*

John Bell

Alexander H. Stephens

George B. McClellan

Robert E. Lee

First Manassas (Bull Run)

William H. Seward

Ulysses S. Grant

Thomas J. (Stonewall) Jackson

Army of Northern Virginia

Shenandoah Valley

Army of Tennessee

Seven Days' Battles

Second Battle of Bull Run

Nathan Bedford Forrest

Anaconda Plan

CHRONOLOGY

1858   William Seward delivers his "Irrepressible Conflict" speech.

1860   Democratic Party splits.

Lincoln elected president.

South Carolina secedes.

United States Army occupies Fort Sumter.

1860–1861   Ten states eventually join South Carolina to create the Confederate States of America.

Jefferson Davis named president of the Confederacy.

Kansas becomes thirty-fourth state.

Fort Sumter falls and Civil War begins.

Union navy blockades southern ports.

Battle of Bull Run.

George McClellan assumes command of the Army of the Potomac.

1862   Ulysses S. Grant's forces take Forts Henry and Donelson.

Battle of the *Virginia* and the *Monitor* marks a major change in naval warfare.

Battle of Shiloh.

Union navy captures New Orleans.

McClellan's peninsular campaign ends with the Seven Days' Battles.

Robert E. Lee assumes command of the Army of Northern Virginia.

Second Battle of Bull Run.

1863   West Virginia becomes the thirty-fifth state.

THEMATIC TOPICS FOR ENRICHMENT

1. What economic stands did the Republicans take in 1860 that attracted northern voters?
2. Give the details of the Crittenden Compromise and explain why both Lincoln and the secessionists rejected the Compromise.
3. In what ways did the Confederate Constitution differ from the United States Constitution?
4. Discuss how Fort Sumter developed into a dilemma for both the Union and the Confederacy.
5. Discuss how each side in the Civil War attempted to finance its participation in the conflict. Why did the Confederacy fail in this regard?
6. Discuss military innovations in the Civil War and how they affected how battles were fought and wars were planned.
7. Explain why Union fortunes were better in western areas in 1862 than they were in the Virginia theater.

GEOGRAPHY OBJECTIVES

1. Assess the sectional character of the 1860 presidential election on a map of the United States (p. 523).
2. Locate the slave states that remained within the Union during the Civil War (p. 523).
3. Identify the states in which the majority of the battles of the Civil War were fought (p. 532).
4. Assess the importance of railroads and rivers in the fighting of the Civil War (p. 532).

SUGGESTED ESSAY TOPICS

1. Why did both national political parties, the Whigs and the Democrats, ultimately split apart in the years leading up to the Civil War?
2. Considering that Lincoln explicitly stated that he was not an abolitionist, why did South Carolina secede from the Union upon his election in 1860?
3. Assess the great difficulty in choosing sides as the Civil War broke out in 1861, particularly for residents of the border states.
4. Compare and contrast Union and Confederate relative advantages in preparing to fight a protracted civil war. What did the Union have to do to win the war? What did the Confederacy need to do to gain its independence?

SUGGESTED WEB ACTIVITY FOR THE CLASSROOM

The Music of the American Civil War

   http://www.pdmusic.org/civilwar.html

This is an extraordinary site. It contains music (in MIDI files) and lyrics to many Civil War era songs. In addition, the site also contains links to many other songs from the 1800s and 1900s. This would work well to load and play the music, showing lyrics simultaneously. A fantastic site!

LECTURE OUTLINE

1. Although Lincoln won a clear electoral majority, the **election of 1860** was in many ways extraordinary; four candidates, Lincoln and Douglas of Illinois, Breckinridge of Kentucky, and Bell of Tennessee, representing three parties, vied for the presidency in what amounted to two separate elections.

    (Show Transparency 15-01: Presidential Election Cartoon, 1860)

    a. Disaffection with the perceived radicalism of the major candidate, William H. Seward, led the Republicans to nominate **Abraham Lincoln,** the favorite son of the Chicago convention.

    b. The nomination of Lincoln and the Republican platform did nothing to quell **southern fears** of the dangers posed by a Republican victory in the upcoming election.

2. Following the electoral college's confirmation of Lincoln's victory, South Carolina led the **Lower South's secession** from the Union.

    (Show Transparency 15-02: Map, Election of 1860 and Southern Secession)

    a. **Northerners affirmed the Union** by publicly supporting Lincoln and declaring secession unconstitutional, but southerners invoked the right of revolution to justify their actions.

    b. In a desperate effort to avert war in the first months of 1861, northerners and southerners floated a number of compromise proposals, most notably that of **John J. Crittenden** of Kentucky—but the time for compromise had passed.

3. Establishment of the **Confederacy** fell to a convention of seceded states that met in Montgomery, Alabama, in the beginning of February.

4. Lincoln brilliantly forced the Confederacy into firing the first shot of the Civil War at **Fort Sumter** on the morning of April 12, 1861.

5. For both states and individuals, **choosing sides** proved an agonizing dilemma with far-ranging consequences.

    (Show Transparency 15-03: Map, Principal Military Campaigns of the Civil War)

    a. In the aftermath of the firing on Fort Sumter, the **border states** were forced to choose sides, with Delaware, Kentucky, and Missouri choosing to remain in the Union.

    b. The Unionist western counties of Virginia seceded from their state in the creation of **West Virginia.**

6. From men to money to materiel, the **balance sheet of war** seemed to favor the Union.

    a. The Union's material advantages would not guarantee victory without **strategy and morale** equal to the daunting task at hand.

    b. The prodigious numbers of volunteers on both sides made initial **mobilization for war** far less difficult than after the fighting had started in earnest.

    c. The bloody engagements of the first years of the Civil War led to a revolution in **weapons and tactics,** particularly as increasingly lethal weapons necessitated new battlefield tactics such as digging trenches and flanking the enemy.

    d. Many contemporaries called the Civil War the first "modern war" because of the incredibly complicated **logistics** involved in amassing, transporting, feeding, arming, supplying, and informing the forces that fought on both sides.

    e. **Financing the war** proved difficult for both sides, with the printing of paper money, new taxes, the sale of war bonds, and various other measures, but overall the North was much more successful than the South.

7. The Civil War was not fought exclusively on land but also with **navies, a blockade, and control of foreign relations,** all of which ultimately proved advantageous for the Union.

   a. The Confederacy mistakenly believed that **King Cotton diplomacy** would be its trump card that would force the English into recognizing the Confederate States of America.

   b. In the **Trent affair** of October 1861, the Union insulted the English and almost pushed them into assisting the Confederacy.

   c. The **Confederate Navy** was composed largely of two purchased British vessels, the *Alabama* and the *Florida*, which captured or sank over 250 Union merchant vessels but which never posed a real threat to the Union's navy.

   d. The *Monitor* **and** *Virginia*, both ironclads, dueled to a draw in their famed March 9, 1862, encounter.

8. The campaigns and battles of 1861–1862 proved that the war would not end quickly, and that only great bloodshed and loss of life would bring the conflict to a conclusion. Battles such as **Shiloh** and **Antietam** cost both sides huge losses of men.

   a. Despite all indications for a smashing Union victory under the command of General George McClellan, the **Battle of Bull Run** on July 21, 1861, turned into a Confederate triumph when Thomas "Stonewall" Jackson's Virginia brigade held its line and General Joseph E. Johnston arrived from the Shenandoah Valley with reinforcements.

   (Show Transparency 15-04: Map, Battle of Bull Run [Manassas], July 21, 1861)

   b. Union **Naval Operations** resulted in a series of victories over Confederate coastal fortifications and the forced surrender of New Orleans at the hands of Admiral David G. Farragut.

   c. Led by Ulysses S. Grant, combined Union forces won key victories at **Fort Henry and Fort Donelson** on the Tennessee and Cumberland rivers.

   (Show Transparency 15-05: Map, Kentucky–Tennessee Theater, Winter–Spring 1862)

   d. Despite Union losses of some 13,000 men in two days of bloody fighting, the Union and Grant defeated Confederate forces at the **Battle of Shiloh** on April 6–7, 1862.

   (Show Transparency 15-06: Map, Battle of Shiloh, April 6–7, 1862)

   e. The Union's fortunes reversed dramatically later in the spring of 1862 in the **Virginia theater,** as Johnston's army put McClellan's Army of the Potomac on the defensive and Jackson's "foot cavalry" wreaked havoc in the Shenandoah Valley.

   f. In the **Seven Days' Battles** at the end of June 1862, Robert E. Lee's Army of Northern Virginia turned the momentum of the war in favor of the Confederacy by driving McClellan's larger force from the outskirts of Richmond back towards the James River.

(Show Transparency 15-07: Maps, Peninsular Campaign, April–May 1862 & Seven Days' Battles, June 25–July 1, 1862)

9. For the remainder of 1862, **Confederate counteroffensives** were designed to break the Union's will to fight, and at the **Second Battle of Bull Run,** the Confederates again demonstrated that Union victory, if it ever were to come, was a far way off.

(Show Transparency 15-08: Map, Second Battle of Manassas [Bull Run], August 29–30, 1862)

Conclusion: The election of Lincoln and the subsequent secession of eleven southern states culminated in Civil War. Neither Lincoln nor any party—North or South—could have predicted in 1860 that within two years the country would be mired in a brutal war without any foreseeable end. Perhaps only a few abolitionists sensed that the war would spell the end of slavery in the United States, but President Lincoln was beginning to reach that same conclusion.

FOCUS ON FEATURES

American Album: Confederate Dead on the Battlefield, p. 550
History Through Film: *The Red Badge of Courage*, p. 536
Link to the Past: The Valley of the Shadow: Two Communities in the Civil War, p. 531

TEACHING RESOURCES

The Civil War—episodes one, two, and three—by Ken Burns offers an award-winning account of the war's beginning and its first two years. PBS Video (99 minutes, 69 minutes, and 76 minutes, respectively).

The Divided Union: The American Civil War is a five-part history of the conflict. Filmic Archives (55 minutes each).

Civil War Journal, Volume I offers a thirteen-episode history of the war from a more personal point of view. Filmic Archives (650 minutes).

Ironclads: The Monitor and the Merrimac covers a turning point in naval history. Filmic Archives (30 minutes).

The Battle of Glorietta Pass: Gettysburg of the West recounts this battle in the West in 1862. Films for the Humanities & Sciences (28 minutes, black and white).

Chapter 16

A New Birth of Freedom, 1862–1865

CHAPTER SUMMARY

When Confederate armies invaded Kentucky and Maryland in the late summer of 1862, northern hopes for a quick end to the war and the restoration of the Union ended. President Lincoln realized that a total war, in which the Union would mobilize every resource at its disposal to crush the Confederacy, was the only option he could pursue. Total war meant, however, that the Union would have to deal with the issue of the abolition of slavery.

In the beginning of the war, Union soldiers fought only to restore the 1860 union of states. Any attempt to make slavery's demise a war goal would have alienated border states and infuriated those Union soldiers who held racist beliefs. As Union armies advanced into slave states, however, thousands of slaves fled their owners and sought sanctuary in army camps. Union commanders soon declared runaways from Confederate sympathizers "contrabands" and refused to return them to their masters. Congress approved of this practice as a war measure, in order to deny Confederates a vital source of labor. By March 1862, the Union forbade the return of any slave who crossed Union lines, even slaves belonging to Unionists.

By the summer of 1862, Lincoln made abolition of slavery the second Union war goal. Growing pressure from within his own party to do something about slavery and the North's desire to crush southern "traitors" forced Lincoln's decision. As commander in chief, Lincoln had the power to order the seizure of enemy property, of which slaves were an integral part. The president shrewdly couched his Emancipation Proclamation in military terms, designed either to end the war or to take from the South its laboring class. At his cabinet's request, Lincoln agreed to issue his proclamation only after a significant northern battlefield victory.

The Confederate invasion of Maryland culminated in the Battle of Antietam (Sharpsburg) on September 17, 1862. The armies of Robert E. Lee and George McClellan fought to a bloody standoff, but Lee's retreat to Virginia gave Lincoln the "victory" that he needed. On September 22, the president issued his preliminary proclamation, stating that rebellious states had until January 1 to cease hostilities or, on that day, all slaves in areas still in rebellion would be freed. Because this was a military measure, slaves in Union states and in former Confederate territory controlled by Union forces would not be affected. Union armies suddenly became armies of liberation.

Military reverses plagued the Union from December 1862 through the spring of 1863. The new Union commander in Virginia, Ambrose Burnside, suffered defeat at the Battle of Fredericksburg, and Ulysses S. Grant's attempts to take Vicksburg on the Mississippi River bogged down. Northern hopes revived briefly with a victory at Stones River (Murfreesboro) on January 2. But in May still another Union general, Joseph Hooker, had his army routed in Virginia by Robert E. Lee's Confederates at the Battle of Chancellorsville.

Northern woes in the winter of 1863 brought increased desertion from Union armies, war weariness from the northern home front, and calls for peace at any price from "Copperheads," a term for northern Democrats. Meanwhile, in the Confederacy, growing economic problems led to food shortages by the spring of 1863, culminating in bread riots in Richmond in April.

Tensions escalated in both the North and the South after both governments passed conscription laws. Dissent grew between social classes in the Confederacy when the government allowed wealthy southerners to avoid the draft by hiring substitutes. Slaveowners or overseers were also exempted if their plantations had twenty or more slaves. The Union conscription law of 1863 provided for substitutes as well, angering northerners unable financially to take advantage of such provisions. Northerners resented the draft not only on racist grounds but on economic ones as well. They believed that working-class men were being drafted in order to free blacks from slavery, and that those blacks would then move north to take white laborers' jobs. Racism of this kind led to the New York City draft riots in July 1863, in which huge mobs destroyed draft offices, looted homes, and lynched several blacks.

The Civil War also altered the roles of American women. While a few on both sides served as spies or disguised themselves as men to serve as soldiers, most worked as clerks, secretaries, and nurses. Women volunteers also organized relief organizations such as the Sanitary Commission. Women's wartime service spurred the nascent women's rights movement to push for equality between the sexes.

Events in mid-1863 made it apparent to many that the high tide for the Confederacy had been Lee's victory at Chancellorsville. Determined to demonstrate the Confederacy's power and perhaps to win recognition from abroad, Lee proposed an invasion of Pennsylvania and led his army northward to the Battle of Gettysburg, the most important battle of the war. From July 1 through July 3, the battle raged between Lee's Army of Northern Virginia and George Meade's Army of the Potomac. On the third day, Lee launched a direct frontal assault on Union lines (Pickett's charge) only to suffer a devastating defeat. The Confederate army's retreat from Pennsylvania marked a turning point in the war. On July 4, Grant's Union forces took Vicksburg. Within a few days, Port Hudson fell as well, giving the Union complete control of the Mississippi River. Confederate fortunes revived briefly with a victory at the Battle of Chickamauga in September. Undaunted, Grant's army broke the siege of Chattanooga in November and routed the Confederates from Missionary Ridge.

Momentum shifted to the Union side, in part due to the efforts of black men fighting in the Union forces. African Americans believed that they were fighting for equal rights for their race. By 1863, the whites-only war ended, as the North enrolled free black men and emancipated slaves in the army and navy. Their officers remained white, but units such as the 54th Massachusetts Infantry proved their valor on the battlefield. Before the war ended, approximately 180,000 African-American males would serve the Union cause.

War weariness returned to the North in the spring and summer of 1864, and Lincoln entered the darkest hours of his presidency. With Grant as general in chief leading the Army of the Potomac in Virginia, the Union advanced closer and closer to Richmond. The North, however, lost thousands of men in the Battles of the Wilderness, Spotsylvania, and Cold Harbor. By autumn, Grant was bogged down in the siege of Petersburg, a railway center south of the Confederate capital. Although William T. Sherman led a Union advance on Atlanta, by the end of July observers began to doubt whether his troops could capture the city.

Democrats hoping to oust Lincoln in the November election called for peace at any price, even independence for the South, and nominated as their presidential candidate General George McClellan. Scrambling for support, the Republicans renamed their party the Union Party and chose a Democrat, Andrew Johnson of Tennessee, as Lincoln's vice presidential running mate. As the casualties mounted from the summer's battles, Lincoln gloomily predicted that he would not be reelected.

The president's political problems dwindled rapidly in the fall of 1864. On September 2, Sherman's troops marched into Atlanta, and a few weeks later, Philip Sheridan's forces routed the Confederates from Virginia's Shenandoah Valley. The Confederacy reeled toward collapse, and Lincoln swamped McClellan in the election.

In November and December, the Confederate plight worsened. The Battles of Franklin and Nashville virtually destroyed the Army of the Tennessee, which was the major Confederate force outside of Virginia. Sherman's famed march across Georgia to Savannah broke the will of many southern people to continue to fight such a formidable enemy, and by early 1865, Sherman's army launched a similar destructive march northward across South and North Carolina. In Virginia, relentless pressure on the Confederate forces caused them to abandon Petersburg and Richmond and retreat westward. On April 9 at Appomattox Court House, Robert E. Lee surrendered his army to Ulysses S. Grant, virtually ending the war. At the cost of four years of fighting and 625,000 lives lost, the nation was preserved and slavery was abolished.

LIBERTY, EQUALITY, POWER: A THEMATIC BRAID

Lincoln's Emancipation Proclamation, even with its limits, effectively marked the end of slavery in America. The Thirteenth Amendment, when finally passed by Congress in January 1865 and ratified by the states in December of that same year, completed what Lincoln's proclamation and the Union forces had started.

The power to end slavery ultimately took the form of a constitutional amendment, but the real power to end slavery had come from the barrel of a gun. Not only did white Union soldiers make the end of slavery a war goal from 1862 onward, but the Union's enrollment of black soldiers and sailors permitted African Americans themselves to contribute to the fight for slavery's end. Their valiant service on the battlefields gave at least a temporary boost to the concept of racial equality.

American women from both North and South expanded their own roles during the war. Economically, the war opened new jobs for women in clerical work and nursing and forced many to assume the operation of farms, plantations, and businesses while men were away at war. Volunteer work to nurse the wounded and sick, to collect bandages and medicine for the armies, and to deliver books and other materials to soldiers drew the efforts of many more women. The dedicated and valuable service of women during the war gave unrealistic hope to women's rights advocates that a grateful nation would reward them with equality of the sexes after the war.

IDENTIFICATIONS

Contrabands
Copperheads
Battle of Antietam
Emancipation Proclamation
Ambrose E. Burnside
Joseph Hooker
Clement L. Vallandigham
Battle of Cedar Creek
Morrill Land-grant College Act
Pacific Railroad Act
United States Sanitary Commission
Battle of Chancellorsville
Pickett's charge
George McClellan
William S. Rosecrans
New York City draft riots
Stonewall Jackson
George Thomas
Port Hudson
Wilderness
Cold Harbor
Horace Greeley
"March to the sea"

Vicksburg
Chickamauga
54th Massachusetts Infantry
Ulysses S. Grant
William T. Sherman
Andersonville Prison
Philip Sheridan
Homestead Act
Appomattox
John Wilkes Booth
Thirteenth Amendment
Battle of Gettysburg
Benjamin Butler
Fredericksburg
Richmond bread riot
Dr. Elizabeth Blackwell
Joseph Johnston
Braxton Bragg
Fort Wagner
Spotsylvania
John Bell Hood
Fort Pillow

CHRONOLOGY

1862	Confederacy enacts conscription.
	Battle of Antietam.
	Lincoln issues the preliminary Emancipation Proclamation.
	Battle of Fredericksburg.
	Homestead Act and Morrill Act pass.
1863	Lincoln signs final Emancipation Proclamation.
	Union enacts conscription.
	Food riots break out in the Confederacy.
	Battle of Chancellorsville.
	Battle of Gettysburg.
	Vicksburg falls to Grant's besieging army.
	Port Hudson surrenders.
	Draft riots erupt in New York City.
1864	Grant becomes the Union's general in chief.
	Battle of the Wilderness.
	Battle of Spotsylvania.
	Atlanta falls to William T. Sherman's army.
	Lincoln wins reelection.
	Sherman begins his march to the sea.
1865	Lee surrenders to Grant at Appomattox (April 9).
	Lincoln is assassinated (April 14).
	Last Confederate army surrenders (June 23).
	Thirteenth Amendment is ratified.

THEMATIC TOPICS FOR ENRICHMENT

1. Explain the writ of *habeas corpus* and why the Lincoln administration suspended it on occasion during the war.

2. Discuss the Clement L. Vallandigham affair and explain how it became an issue of treason versus freedom of speech.

3. Why are the Battle of Gettysburg and the fall of Vicksburg often considered the turning point of the Civil War?

4. Discuss how black men became involved in the Union war effort and how they fared.

5. Describe how each side handled prisoners of war and how treatment of prisoners became a major controversy.

6. Why did General Sherman march across Georgia, and what were the results of his campaign?

GEOGRAPHY OBJECTIVES

1. Discuss the errors made by both Confederate and Union commanders at the Battle of Antietam. Why was this battle, essentially a draw, still of extreme importance (p. 563)?

2. Illustrate Hooker's plans in 1863. Then explain how Robert E. Lee and Stonewall Jackson combined to foil those plans. (p. 574).

3. Identify the following locations, and note what occurred therein and/or thereby: Cemetery Hill, the Angle, Little Round Top, Devil's Den, Pickett's charge (p. 575).

4. Illustrate three different ways in which Ulysses S. Grant attempted to take Vicksburg. Use it further to explain fully why the final attempt in the summer of 1863 proved successful where the others had failed (p. 577).

5. Trace the course of the war in Tennessee and northern Georgia from the Battle of Stones River through Union victory at Missionary Ridge (p. 578).

6. Illustrate Grant's strategy in the Wilderness campaign. Explain his major errors. Note also ways in which Grant's campaign differed from the earlier ones of Hooker, Burnside, or even McClellan (p. 584).

7. In what ways does the map on page 586 help explain why Jefferson Davis replaced Joseph Johnston with John Bell Hood? In what ways do the inset maps on the same page indicate that this may have been a mistake?

8. Trace the path of Hood's forces from Atlanta to Nashville. What was the purpose of this campaign? Why did it fail (p. 591)?

SUGGESTED ESSAY TOPICS

1. Trace the course of the military campaign in the Eastern Theater from Antietam to Appomattox, noting key battles and Union command changes as you go.

2. Discuss the impact of the war on the Union and Confederate "home fronts." Note economic issues, draft policy, and the roles of women.

3. Explain the considerations that led Lincoln to issue the Emancipation Proclamation. Discuss its overall impact on the war effort. Why do you think this document is so often misunderstood?

4. Choose two of the following battles for discussion. Include major elements of each conflict, including commanders, size of armies, advantages and disadvantages for each side, maneuvers, outcome, and especially *significance* of the battles: First Bull Run, Shiloh, Antietam, Gettysburg, and Vicksburg.

SUGGESTED WEB ACTIVITY FOR THE CLASSROOM

Letters Home from the Civil War—Civil War Archive

http://www.civilwararchive.com/LETTERS/letters.htm

This is part of a site containing numerous entries and links. The letters here provide keen insight into soldiers' experiences. They also illustrate a wide variety of writing abilities, and would make excellent discussion starters.

LECTURE OUTLINE

1. Lincoln's decision to issue an emancipation proclamation led directly to a **new birth of freedom,** while it radically enlarged the scope and purpose of the war and raised difficult questions concerning the future of the Union.

2. Both sides initially tried to sidestep the **issue of slavery,** but as time passed many northerners came to see a strike against it as a means of defeating the South.

    a. Slaves themselves helped force the issue by "voting with their feet" and fleeing to Union lines, where they were allowed to remain, on grounds that they were **"contraband"** of war.

    b. Lincoln's efforts to persuade border state leaders to accept **"compensated emancipation"** met with obstinance and failure.

    c. Slave-owner recalcitrance and calls from various advisors for tougher action led Lincoln to make a **decision for presidential emancipation.**

        (Show Transparency 16-01: Cartoon, "Abe Lincoln's Last Card," 1862)

        i. Lincoln further reasoned that emancipation would enhance northern resolve and be well received by foreign nations.

        ii. Lincoln made his decision in July 1862 but was advised to **wait until** his armies had scored a **military success,** lest the policy look like a move of desperation.

    d. Lincoln called for 300,000 **new federal troops** and 300,000 more militiamen in the summer of 1862.

    e. General Lee, following up on his victory at Second Bull Run, came north in September in a campaign that climaxed at the **Battle of Antietam.**

        (Show Transparency 16-03: Map, Lee's Invasion of Maryland, 1862; and Battle of Antietam, September 17, 1862)

        i. Numerous things went wrong for the Confederates; most notably, a copy of **Lee's orders** was found and given to General McClellan.

        ii. 23,000 combined casualties made September 17, 1862, the **bloodiest single day of the war.**

    f. Though in many ways a draw, Lee's forces had retreated. The Union claimed victory, and Lincoln issued the **Emancipation Proclamation,** freeing slaves in states still "in rebellion" as of January 1, 1863.

3. Several developments made 1862–1863 a **winter of discontent.**

    a. Antietam encouraged Lincoln to remove McClellan. His replacement, Ambrose Burnside, launched a frontal assault on the heights of **Fredericksburg** that was repulsed with heavy casualties, and in the western theater Grant bogged down in his attempt to capture Vicksburg.

    b. Lincoln's popularity plummeted, and the **Copperheads,** antiwar northern Democrats, called for the cessation of hostilities and recognition of southern independence.

    c. While the North struggled with low morale, southerners faced chronic food shortages, which at times exploded into **food riots.**

    d. In both the South (1862) and North (1863), wartime drafts were met with contempt by poorer elements, many of whom resented exemptions afforded the wealthy.

        i. Southern **plantation owners were often excused** so as to keep watch over the slaves and prevent uprisings.

        ii. **Wealthy northerners could avoid the draft** by simply paying $300.00 as a commutation fee.

    e. Closer historical examination, however, reveals that the war was **not exclusively a poor man's fight.**

4. The 37th Congress enacted three laws, which provided what historians have called a **blueprint for modern America.**

    a. The **Homestead Act** granted farmers 160-acre homesteads virtually free, provided they lived thereon for five years and improved the land.

b. The **Morrill Land-grant College Act** gave states thousands of acres of land with which to establish colleges.

c. The **Pacific Railroad Act** granted land and loans to railroad companies to encourage the growth of transcontinental lines.

d. The war also offered many **opportunities to women**—thus bolstering the fledgling women's rights movement.

    i. Their most notable achievement was likely the formation of the **United States Sanitary Commission,** which supplied nurses to army hospitals.

    ii. Some women served in war industries, others joined the civil service, still more served as spies, and **some actually enlisted** (posing as men).

5. The summer of 1863 is often considered the **high tide of the Confederacy.**

a. Lee's defeat of Joseph Hooker at **Chancellorsville** in May owed to Lee's bold, aggressive action in the face of Hooker's negligence.

    (Show Transparency 16-04: Map, Battle of Chancellorsville, May 2–6, 1863)

b. Another Confederate invasion of the North climaxed on July 1–3, 1863, when Lee's army clashed with that of Hooker's replacement, George Meade, at **Gettysburg,** the greatest battle in American history.

    (Show Transparency 16-05: Map, Battle of Gettysburg, July 1–3, 1863)

    i. Thrice Lee attempted to dislodge Union forces from a series of hills east of the town—first attacking the northern and southern ends of the line and then assaulting the center in the quixotic and disastrous **Pickett's charge.**

    ii. In three days of fighting, 50,000 men became casualties. Lee's army limped back to Virginia, halfheartedly pursued by Union troops.

c. Grant's successful conclusion of the **Vicksburg campaign** coincided with Lee's retreat from Gettysburg, and the Union gained full control of the vital Mississippi waterway.

    (Show Transparency 16-06: Map, Vicksburg Campaign, April–July 1863)

d. Just a few months later, in September, Union forces under William Rosecrans launched major campaigns in Tennessee and Georgia.

    i. With reinforcements from the Army of Northern Virginia, Braxton Bragg was able to spring a trap on Rosecrans at **Chickamauga** Creek near **Chattanooga.**

    (Show Transparency 16-07: Map, Road to Chickamauga, June–September 1863)

    ii. Lincoln reinforced Chattanooga with troops from Virginia and the Vicksburg campaign and **brought in Grant,** who drove Confederate forces off the surrounding heights in November.

    iii. These successes convinced Lincoln to appoint Grant commander in chief of the Union forces in March 1864.

6. The Emancipation Proclamation had reinforced calls for the enlistment of **black men in the Union armies.**

a. Initially envisioned as garrison and labor forces, black regiments would themselves **push for the opportunity of combat.**

    i. In May and June 1863, black troops fought well in the campaign for **Port Hudson.**

    ii. The **54th Massachusetts** gallantly assaulted Fort Wagner (South Carolina) that July, suffering 50 percent casualties in a failed effort that nevertheless brought widespread praise.

b. Continued military victories were the principal factors in **confirming emancipation policies** as a permanent policy.

7. Many southerners succumbed to defeatism during the trying winter of 1863–1864. More would do so in the following **"year of decision."**

   a. Confederate armies continued to resist, hoping that a **war of attrition** could tap antiwar sentiments, weaken northern wills, and prompt voters to oust Lincoln in the 1864 election in favor of a "peace Democrat."

   b. Grant, now general in chief, struck southward from Washington in early May. In two days of hellish fighting, the Confederates inflicted severe casualties on Grant's forces in the **Wilderness.**

(Show Transparency 16-08: Map, Battle of the Wilderness and Spotsylvania, May 5–12, 1864)

   c. Unlike earlier commanders, **Grant did not retreat.** Instead, he regrouped and again attempted to outflank Lee.
      i. In mid-May, assaults against Confederate entrenchments at **Spotsylvania** again produced high casualties, more Union than Confederate.
      ii. On June 3, an ill-advised assault at **Cold Harbor** led to Union casualties reminiscent of Gettysburg.

   d. Grant eventually settled into what would become a nine-month siege of Petersburg, Virginia, having suffered **65,000 total casualties** since May, while elsewhere in the state a **stalemate** prevailed.

   e. In Georgia, **William Tecumseh Sherman** gradually pushed Joseph E. Johnston's forces back toward Atlanta.
      i. An impatient Jefferson Davis replaced Johnston with **John Bell Hood,** who launched three futile offensives, severely weakening his forces.
      ii. Sherman placed **Atlanta under siege.**

(Show Transparency 16-09: Map, Campaign for Atlanta, May–September 1864)

   f. The Confederate attrition strategy seemed to be working, evidenced not only by Democratic opposition but also by **growing dissent** among the Republicans.
      i. In the presidential contest, the **Democrats nominated George McClellan,** who called for an immediate cessation of hostilities.
      ii. **Lincoln himself despaired** that he would be badly beaten in his attempt at reelection unless something changed drastically, but he refused to compromise on emancipation.

   g. Controversy over **prisoners of war** was further complicating matters for Lincoln.
      i. The most ghastly example of their suffering came at **Andersonville,** a "hellhole" in which prisoners died at a rate of more that one per day.
      ii. Lincoln and Grant resisted southern offers of **prisoner exchanges** until early 1865, however, largely because the South refused to include black troops in the proposals.

   h. A desperate Confederacy decided to **recruit slaves to fight,** but the war ended before any such regiments were organized.

8. An improved military situation eventually ensured the **reelection of Lincoln and the end of the Confederacy.**

   a. Sherman's **capture of Atlanta** from Hood's depleted forces in September was both a symbolic and substantive victory.

   b. Further Union success came in the **Shenandoah Valley.**
      i. Philip Sheridan sought not only to drive Jubal Early's forces from the valley but also to **deprive the Confederacy** of the area's resources.
      ii. Sheridan's men thoroughly destroyed the region and routed Early in a series of battles, climaxing at **Cedar Creek** in October.

© 2002 Thomson Learning, Inc.

   c. **The Confederate leadership resolved to keep fighting,** but Sherman resolved to convince them otherwise.

   d. **Sherman marched southward** 280 miles from Atlanta to Savannah, his 60,000 men wrecking almost everything in their path.

   e. Hood marched his forces northward, where he sacrificed the bulk of his men in attacks at **Franklin and Nashville** before resigning in defeat.

   f. The capture of **Fort Fisher** in January 1865 closed the Confederacy's last open port (Wilmington, North Carolina).

(Show Transparency 16-10: Map, Hood's Tennessee Campaign, October–November 1864; and Nashville, December 15–16, 1864)

   g. Sherman's forces headed **northward through the Carolinas,** inflicting even more destruction than they had wrought in Georgia.

   h. Grant, meanwhile, finally pressured Lee out of Richmond and Petersburg. Lee fled westward, only to have his remnant force cornered near **Appomattox.** On April 9, 1865, Lee surrendered.

(Show Transparency 16-02: Graph, Comparative Strength of Union and Confederate Armies)

   i. Northern celebrations soon turned to mourning, however, following the **assassination of Lincoln** on April 14.

Conclusion: The Civil War resolved two fundamental issues. The first confirmed the superiority of federal authority to that of the states, and the second assured the elimination of slavery. Such resolution came at a cost of over 600,000 lives. At the same time, a power shift from South to North took place in the reconstructed Union that would hold for the next half century.

FOCUS ON FEATURES

American Album: The Fruits of War, p. 581
History Through Film: *Glory*, p. 582
Link to the Past: The United States Sanitary Commission, p. 573

TEACHING RESOURCES

The Civil War—episodes four through nine—by Ken Burns offers an award-winning account of the war's middle and closing years. PBS Video (62 minutes, 95 minutes, 70 minutes, 72 minutes, 69 minutes, and 68 minutes, respectively).

The Red Badge of Courage is a feature film of Stephen Crane's classic novel, directed by John Huston and starring Audie Murphy. Filmic Archives (69 minutes).

Smithsonian's *Great Battles of the Civil War* is a six-part series that offers narration by James M. McPherson and documentation of each major battle of the war. Filmic Archives.

Royal Federal Blues provides the most comprehensive account of African-American participation in the Civil War. Filmic Archives (30 minutes).

Lincoln is a four-part series about the president. Filmic Archives (240 minutes total).

Great Generals of the South focuses on Robert E. Lee and Stonewall Jackson. Filmic Archives (60 minutes).

The Massachusetts 54th Colored Infantry illustrates the compelling story of African Americans' devotion to the Union as well as remarkable heroism. PBS Video (60 minutes).

Glory is a feature film, starring Denzel Washington, about the 54th Massachusetts Infantry. Filmic Archives (120 minutes).

Chapter 17

RECONSTRUCTION, 1863–1877

CHAPTER SUMMARY

From the earliest days of the Civil War, the North had been fighting to "reconstruct" the Union. By December 1863, President Lincoln had developed an amnesty and Reconstruction plan for the nation. Lincoln offered amnesty to most Confederates—exceptions being high-ranking civilian and military officials, who were required to take a loyalty oath to the United States and accept the end of slavery. When 10 percent of a state's voters (by 1860 counts) had taken the oath of loyalty, a new state government could be established. Louisiana, Arkansas, and Tennessee—states the Union Army controlled—set out to follow Lincoln's plan.

This swift and mild Reconstruction plan, however, greatly upset radical Republicans, such as Thaddeus Stevens and Charles Sumner, who sought political rights for blacks and demanded that southerners pay for the rebellion. Furthermore, many congressional Republicans insisted that Reconstruction was a legislative matter, not the business of the president. They answered Lincoln's plan with the Wade–Davis Bill of July 1864, a plan calling for a tougher amnesty policy. Lincoln's pocket veto of the bill deepened the division within his own party and made Reconstruction more problematic.

Before the president could issue further Reconstruction policies, the war ended and Lincoln was assassinated. The new president, Andrew Johnson, at first seemed ready to endorse the radical Republican views on Reconstruction, but in May 1865, he offered his own. Like his predecessor, Johnson proposed amnesty to most former Confederates through the use of the loyalty oath. Exceptions to this general amnesty were, again, the highest-ranking Confederate leaders, but to this group Johnson added a new category: anyone who owned taxable property worth $20,000 or more—in other words, wealthy plantation owners. Such people, whom Johnson blamed for causing the war, would receive amnesty only by making a personal application to Johnson himself. To implement each state's Reconstruction, Johnson proposed to appoint a provisional governor who would call for an election of delegates to draw up a new state constitution. Only those white men who had received amnesty could vote or serve as delegates. The new constitution had to repudiate the Confederacy and comply with the U.S. Constitution.

To the growing dismay of moderate and radical Republicans, southern whites in the summer and fall of 1865 followed the parts of Johnson's plan that they liked and ignored the parts they disliked. Southern defiance seemed on the verge of becoming southern rebellion once again. Johnson undermined his own plan by pardoning thousands of former Confederate leaders and plantation owners. Southern voters then horrified northerners by electing some former leaders of the rebellion to Congress.

The fear that southern whites planned to re-enslave blacks arose when the new state legislatures began to enact Black Codes in the fall of 1865. While granting some new rights to former slaves, these laws imposed a second-class citizenship on blacks, denying them the ability to vote, to serve on a jury, to testify against whites, and, in one state, to own land. The codes' definition of vagrancy enabled whites to force blacks to work on farms and plantations, creating a situation that seemed very much like slavery.

The federal agency known as the Freedmen's Bureau was already active in dealing with southern labor and racial problems. Created in March 1865, its purpose was to ease the transition of blacks and whites from a system of slavery to one of free labor. It provided protection to former slaves, set up and supervised labor contracts between whites and blacks, and attempted, in a variety of ways, to reconstruct the southern economy and end the postwar chaos. Private agencies, such as missionary groups from the North, also offered aid to former slaves by setting up schools and hiring teachers to staff them.

When Congress reconvened in December 1865, the Republican majority refused to seat the representatives elected under Johnson's Reconstruction plan and struck at the Black Codes by strengthening the Freedmen's Bureau's power to set them aside. To protect blacks further, Congress passed the Civil Rights Act of

1866, which gave them citizenship and equal protection under the law. Johnson's vetoes of the new Freedmen's Bureau bill and the Civil Rights Act—and Congress's override of these vetoes—revealed not only a deep rift between president and Congress but also a threat to any presidential control over Reconstruction.

In the culmination of this first battle with the president, Congress created its own Reconstruction policies in the form of the Fourteenth Amendment. In addition to giving citizenship to former slaves, the proposed amendment prohibited states from depriving "any person of life, liberty, or property without due process of law" and from denying to any person "the equal protection of the laws." Other provisions urged southern states to give black males the vote, disqualified ex-Confederate leaders from holding office, repudiated the Confederate war debt, and gave Congress power to enforce the amendment. When Tennessee ratified the Fourteenth Amendment, the only one of the former Confederate states to do so, Congress pronounced it reconstructed.

White race riots in the summer of 1866 and Johnson's own clumsy campaigning on behalf of congressional candidates ensured the collapse of presidential Reconstruction and paved the way for Congress's more complete plan. Issued in March 1867, Congress's plan re-imposed military control over the remaining ten unreconstructed states, ordered generals to register voters for elections to choose delegates to state constitutional conventions, enfranchised all males over age twenty-one, and disfranchised (temporarily) former Confederate leaders. When a state ratified the Fourteenth Amendment and adopted a new constitution giving equal political rights to all adult males and civil rights to all citizens, civilian rule would be restored and newly elected congressional representatives would be seated. This plan brought the Republican Party into power in the South, infuriating former southern leaders who soon charged that the new state governments were being run by "carpetbaggers" (northerners), "scalawags" (southern white Unionists), and former slaves ("Negro rule").

The power struggle between the president and Congress climaxed when Johnson challenged the Tenure of Office Act, which had taken away his power to fire his own cabinet officials. The House impeached Johnson in February 1868 on violation of this law and for failing to maintain the proper relationship between Congress and the presidency. Johnson's lawyers exploited a loophole in the Tenure of Office Act and forced senators to consider removing the president because of his failure to cooperate with Congress. By one vote, Johnson escaped removal from office.

Despite white opposition, and even violence from groups such as the Ku Klux Klan, new state governments in the South pressed forward with reforms that included universal male suffrage and the creation of statewide public education. For states that refused to implement the congressional plan, ratification of the Fifteenth Amendment became an additional requirement for Reconstruction after its passage by Congress in 1869. This constitutional change prohibited states from using race, color, or previous condition of servitude as a reason for withholding voting rights.

Ulysses S. Grant won the presidential election in 1868, marking the beginning of the end for Reconstruction policies. During Grant's two terms, corruption flourished inside and outside his administration. Scandals involving Grant's close friends, cabinet officials, members of Congress, and state and local political leaders, shocked (and titillated) the nation. Financial fluctuations and speculation brought on the Panic of 1873, a depression that lasted until 1878. Cries for civil service reform arose, leading finally to the passage of the Pendleton Act in 1883.

Racist and violent southern whites continued to fight against Republican control in the South. Despite efforts to crack down on violence by white supremacists, Congress restored political rights to former Confederate leaders, and Grant continued to withdraw federal troops from the South. The Democratic Party came into power once again, and former slaves feared that the right to vote and other newfound rights were imperiled. With the so-called Compromise of 1877 (a political deal brokered to settle the disputed election of 1876), the Republicans turned over to the Democrats the remaining southern states that they controlled, in return for continued Republican control of the presidency. The Supreme Court's narrow interpretation of Reconstruction laws and amendments further signaled that Reconstruction was over, and northerners virtually left southern blacks to the mercy of their white counterparts for the next eighty years.

LIBERTY, EQUALITY, POWER: A THEMATIC BRAID

The question of power arose in the era of Reconstruction concerning how to give political and economic power to former slaves. Also problematic was how to prevent former Confederates from regaining power and, possibly, starting a new rebellion. Republicans believed that barring former Confederate leaders from office and enfranchising black adult males would give former slaves the political clout to protect themselves. With white allies, blacks would have the power to give the Republican Party control of the South—the only sure way of preventing another rebellion. Eventually, these ideas took the form of the Fourteenth and Fifteenth Amendments, which became the cornerstones of not only Reconstruction but also protection of the individual from state abuses of civil rights.

From their cavalier attitude toward Johnson's Reconstruction plan, to the passage of Black Codes and resistance to congressional Reconstruction policies, southern whites showed that they deeply resented the shift in social and political power that Reconstruction seemed to provide. They fought back with propaganda ("Negro rule," "carpetbaggers," "scalawags") and violence (Ku Klux Klan, Knights of the White Camellia, etc.).

The establishment of the Freedmen's Bureau and the ratification of the Fourteenth and Fifteenth Amendments marked an enormous gain in federal power at the expense of the states. The bureau was arguably the first national welfare agency, and the amendments put the federal government into position to protect the civil liberties of the individual from state abuse.

The other power struggle of the era was between the executive and legislative branches of the federal government. Each claimed the power to control Reconstruction, but Congress ultimately gained the advantage by refusing to seat men elected to Congress under the presidential plan and by impeaching Andrew Johnson. The Senate's refusal to remove Johnson from office revealed that many senators were uneasy about changing the balance of power among the branches of the federal government, but Congress still emerged from the impeachment trial firmly in control of Reconstruction. Within a few years, however, Congress echoed the sentiments of many northerners by retreating from Reconstruction policies and leaving southern blacks in the hands of the white majority—ensuring, in effect, that blacks would not have true liberty or equality for at least the next eighty years.

IDENTIFICATIONS

Proclamation of Reconstruction	Amnesty and Whiskey Ring
William Marcy Tweed	Thaddeus Stevens
Crédit Mobilier	Radical Republicans
Pendleton Act	Charles Sumner
Treaty of Washington (1871)	Wade–Davis Bill
carpetbaggers	Black Codes
scalawags	Freedmen's Bureau
"Negro rule"	sharecropper
"40 acres and a mule"	Fourteenth Amendment
Tenure of Office Act	Edwin M. Stanton
Mississippi Plan	Ku Klux Klan
"Bulldozing"	Hamburg Massacre
Samuel J. Tilden	Fifteenth Amendment
Rutherford B. Hayes	Ulysses S. Grant

Compromise of 1877   Jay Cooke

Horace Greeley   Colfax Massacre

Reconstruction Acts of 1867   National Union Party

Andrew Johnson

CHRONOLOGY

1863	Lincoln announces his Reconstruction plan.
1864	Wade–Davis Bill passed by Congress; Lincoln kills it through pocket veto.
	Freedmen's Bureau established by Congress.
	Lincoln is assassinated.
	Andrew Johnson becomes president.
	Johnson issues his Reconstruction plan and readmits the rest of the former Confederate states to the Union.
	Southern states enact Black Codes.
1866	Freedmen's Bureau extended and given more power.
	Congress approves Fourteenth Amendment.
	Race riots in Memphis and New Orleans.
	Republicans increase their majority in congressional elections.
1867	Congressional Reconstruction plan is passed over Johnson's veto.
1868	Most southern states are readmitted to Congress under the congressional plan.
	Andrew Johnson impeached but not convicted.
	Fourteenth Amendment ratified.
	Ulysses S. Grant wins election as president.
1869	Congress passes the Fifteenth Amendment, which is ratified in 1870.
1871	Ku Klux Klan Act enacted.
1872	Liberal Republicans defect from party.
	Grant wins reelection.
1873	Economic depression begins with the Panic.
1875	"Whiskey Ring" and other scandals befoul Grant administration.
1877	Rutherford B. Hayes becomes president.
	Compromise of 1877.

THEMATIC TOPICS FOR ENRICHMENT

1. How did Andrew Johnson's background, especially his experiences as a prewar politician, affect his Reconstruction position? In what way were Radical Reconstructionists in the Congress surprised by his actions?

2. Discuss the Black Codes, and explain why Republicans found them so objectionable.

© 2002 Thomson Learning, Inc.

3. Explain the role of the Freedmen's Bureau in the South and discuss the labor and racial problems with which it tried to deal.

4. Why did Congress and Andrew Johnson part ways on Reconstruction policies? What events in early 1866 worsened relations between the two?

5. Discuss the provisions of the Fourteenth Amendment and explain why the amendment became such an important guarantor of civil rights.

6. Discuss the events leading to the impeachment of Andrew Johnson. Why did the Senate fail to remove him from office?

7. Discuss the role of the Ku Klux Klan and other terrorist groups during Reconstruction.

8. Discuss the Compromise of 1877 and explain why it marked the end of Reconstruction.

GEOGRAPHY OBJECTIVES

1. With reference to the map on page 610, note the only state to have a black majority at its constitutional convention. Which state had equal representation of whites and blacks?

2. With further reference to the text of pages 615–616, discuss how the map on page 610 challenges notions of the southern Republicans as being a predominantly black party.

3. As you examine the map on page 614, note how the Reconstruction experience of Tennessee differed dramatically from those of the other southern states. Be sure to consult the text concerning how the Fourteenth and Fifteenth Amendments fit into this equation.

4. Use the map on page 625 to compute what the final vote tallies would have been, if any of the three "disputed" states (Florida, Louisiana, South Carolina) had been counted for Tilden. Then, perhaps with reference to the map on page 610, note the final vote count if southern Republicans were not "bulldozed" out of power. Finally, discuss the importance of New York to Tilden's claims. Why, do you think, did New York vote Democratic?

SUGGESTED ESSAY TOPICS

1. Compare and contrast the Reconstruction policies (noting attitudes toward both former slaves and ex-Confederates) of Abraham Lincoln, Andrew Johnson, and the Radical Republicans.

2. Describe southern attitudes toward Reconstruction as imposed on them under the Republican Congress. In what ways did southerners protest Reconstruction policies? Explain the political situation that brought Reconstruction to an end.

3. Explain what was meant by the terms "carpetbagger," "scalawag," and "Negro rule." How true was the propaganda against Republican-controlled governments in the southern states?

4. Assess U.S. Grant's two terms as president. What did he accomplish? What were his failures?

SUGGESTED WEB ACTIVITY FOR THE CLASSROOM

American Slave Narratives: An Online Anthology

http://xroads.virginia.edu/~HYPER/wpa/wpahome.html

During the 1930s, the Works Progress Administration (WPA) sponsored a national Writers' Project designed to put people to work while at the same time recording the life experiences of many Americans. The

Slave Narratives are perhaps the best known of these oral histories. This site contains excerpts from more than a dozen interviews, several with sound excerpts. The presentation is highly effective. Newspaper articles or other historical materials sometimes accompany the interviews. The presentation here truly brings oral history to life.

LECTURE OUTLINE

1. From the beginning of the Civil War, the North fought with **Reconstruction** in mind. The precise meaning of that word, however, varied among individuals, and changed as the war progressed.

2. Lincoln's **Proclamation of Amnesty and Reconstruction** seemed, to many Republicans, both too lenient toward former Confederates and insufficient in guaranteeing the rights and liberties of former slaves.

   a. When the occupied Confederate state government of Louisiana reorganized under this plan, its new legislature denied blacks the vote and enacted restrictive labor laws that **seemed a veritable return to slavery.**

   (Show Transparency 17-01: Thomas Nast Cartoon, "This Is a White Man's Government," 1868)

   b. Radical Republicans came to support tougher policies epitomized in the **Wade–Davis Bill,** which Lincoln opposed.

3. **Andrew Johnson** became president upon Lincoln's assassination, and Radical Republicans mistakenly thought he would prove cooperative.

   a. Johnson expressed no love for the planter class but was a **white supremacist** who aimed to deny blacks the fruits of Reconstruction.
      i. Under Johnson's plans, the southern states defiantly **elected prominent Confederate officials** to office.
      ii. Johnson also granted **special pardons** to many of those "aristocrats" whom he had earlier vowed to punish.

   b. Even more alarming to Radical Republicans was the establishment of the **Black Codes,** which relegated blacks to second-class citizenship.

   c. The war had left the **southern economy** in chaos. Planters had no labor, and ex-slaves often had neither land nor work.

   d. The **Freedmen's Bureau** sought to establish labor contracts between landowners and the former slaves.
      i. Proposals to provide **land for the landless** through confiscation of plantations failed to reach fruition.
      ii. Eventually, a new system of **sharecropping** emerged.

   e. The Freedmen's Bureau was more successful in providing **educational opportunities for blacks.**

4. By the time Congress met in late 1865, the Republican majority had resolved to challenge Johnson with **new Reconstruction policies.**

   a. **Johnson showed contempt** for Congressional initiatives.

   b. Congress passed a civil rights bill and another expanding the Freedmen's Bureau's powers, **overriding presidential vetoes.**

   c. More dramatically, Congress sent to the states the **Fourteenth Amendment,** which vastly expanded federal powers to prevent state violations of civil rights.

d. Johnson's obstinacy and courting of disgraced Democrats were pivotal factors in a sweeping radical Republican victory in the **1866 congressional elections.**

e. Given a three-to-one majority, the Republican Congress passed the **Reconstruction Acts of 1867.**
    i. They enfranchised black males, disfranchised certain ex-Confederates, and sent the army south for **enforcement,** dividing the southern states into five military districts until they accepted the Fourteenth Amendment.
    ii. Some **735,000 enfranchised black voters** became the backbone of the Republican Party in the South, which took control of southern state governments.

5. Johnson did everything he could to stop Congressional Reconstruction, provoking considerable ire. His firing of the Secretary of War was the final straw, which convinced the House to vote for **impeachment.**

   a. A few Republicans were persuaded to **acquit** the president, sparing him from impeachment **by one vote.** Johnson was left politically impotent, however.

   b. **Majority Republican state conventions** enacted universal male suffrage and mandated statewide public schools for both races.

   c. With ratification of the **Fifteenth Amendment** in 1870, the Constitution became color-blind for the first time in history, but advocates of women's rights, disillusioned by their exclusion, founded their own suffrage association.

   d. War hero Ulysses S. Grant, who had openly broken with Johnson, won the **1868 election.**

(Show Transparency 17-02: Map, Black and White Participation in Constitutional Conventions, 1867–1868)

6. The **Grant administration** is usually branded a failure, owing to widespread corruption among presidential subordinates.

   a. In reality, several government agencies made real progress in establishing a more professional and qualified **civil service.**

   b. The administration also achieved some **foreign policy** success by ameliorating tensions with Great Britain and Canada.

   c. While the Fifteenth Amendment seemed to many a victory for Reconstruction, there was no **peace in the South.**

   d. Blacks comprised 80 percent of southern Republican voters yet held only 15 to 20 percent of elected positions. The **myth of "ignorant" black politicians** is patently false.

   e. **Carpetbaggers** (northern whites who moved to the South) did occupy a disproportionate number of political offices, but most were businessmen bent on modernizing the South, not unscrupulous scavengers, as southern myths would have it.

   f. **Scalawags** (southern native white Republicans) came largely from areas with traditional hostility to the southern planter aristocracy.

(Show Transparency 17-03: Map, Reconstruction in the South)

   g. The most potent weapon of the Democrat arsenal was violence, epitomized by the **Ku Klux Klan** and similar racist organizations.
    i. One Klan goal was to keep blacks consigned to second-class citizenship. The **burning of schools** and whippings of "uppity" blacks were manifestations of this intent.
    ii. The Klan also strove to destroy the Republican Party by **terrorizing voters.**
    iii. Militias, federal troops, and new federal laws had only limited success against the Klan.

   h. Grant staved off the challenge of "Liberal Republican" Horace Greeley to win **reelection in 1872,** but Greeley's calls to abandon Reconstruction struck a responsive chord with many northerners.

      i.   To make matters worse, **panic on Wall Street in 1873** plunged the economy into a five-year recession.

7. Economic anguish, and a growing weariness with the seemingly endless turmoil of southern politics, turned many northern voters against Republican Party politics and prompted **retreat from Reconstruction.**

    a. Democratic tactics of coercing white Republicans and intimidating black voters conquered the **Mississippi election of 1875.**

    b. The **Supreme Court,** meanwhile, ruled against many aspects of civil rights legislation, even challenging some aspects of the Fourteenth and Fifteenth Amendments via its narrow interpretation.

    c. The **election of 1876** between Democrat Samuel Tilden and Republican Rutherford B. Hayes took place amidst Democratic attempts to "bulldoze" black voters into submission.

    d. The candidates polled nearly equal votes, with Tilden commanding a small lead in the popular vote, but three southern states experienced **disputed returns** owing to widespread "bulldozing," and the election hung in limbo.

    e. Congress had to appoint a special committee to break the deadlock, which it accomplished by hammering out the **Compromise of 1877.**

        i.   To avert crisis, the Republicans agreed to provide economic help to the South and to **end "bayonet rule."**

       ii. The Democrats agreed to accept **Hayes as president.**

    f. Without federal troop support, the southern Republican Party collapsed. Thus the Compromise marks the **end of Reconstruction.**

Conclusion: Reconstruction had both reincorporated the former Confederate states into the Union and destroyed slavery. But continued inequities relegated the newly freed slaves into second-class citizenship, wherein most would remain for nearly another century. The Compromise of 1877 signaled the willingness of northerners to let the South go its own way, at least for the present.

FOCUS ON FEATURES

American Album: Cartoons for Freedom, p. 620
History Through Film: *Birth of a Nation*, p. 616
Link to the Past: African-American Odyssey: Quest for Full Citizenship, p. 606

TEACHING RESOURCES

Opening of the West is a documentary on Reconstruction and westward expansion. Filmic Archives (53 minutes).

America Grows Up covers the period from 1850 to c. 1900, focusing on manufacturing, foreign policy, and the shift from a rural to an urban society. Filmic Archives (53 minutes).

The Klan: A Legacy of Hate in America provides an overview of the first 120 years of the organization. Filmic Archives (30 minutes).

The Iron Road details the building and completion of the transcontinental railroad. PBS Video (60 minutes).

CORE CONCEPT
LECTURE LAUNCHERS VIDEO
INSTRUCTOR'S GUIDE

INTRODUCTION

Harcourt's Core Concept Lecture Launchers video package to accompany *Liberty, Equality, Power: A History of the American People* is an innovative teaching tool created so that students can learn by connecting the written word with visual images. The two videos that comprise our package do not replace the textbook; they enhance key text concepts. The subjects selected for the videos relate directly to the underlying theme of the textbook, liberty, equality, power, and how these concepts interact to drive the American experience. With this goal in mind, we selected 16 topics that fit our criteria and serve to "flesh out" central issues raised in the textbook.

These subjects appear as video segments, arranged chronologically with eight segments on each video. Several topics that have a close relationship to the central theme of the textbook receive special emphasis. Chief among these are the issues of slavery and the African-American struggle for liberty and equality; the Constitution and the never-ending endeavors to find the proper balance of power that will ensure liberty and equality for all citizens; and the continual influx of immigrants and the movements of migrants in their attempts to acquire liberty, equality, and security in a new home.

One video covers American history up to 1877, and the second examines America since 1863. *Liberty, Equality, Power* contains five sections, and the videos conform loosely to these sections. This parallel structure allowed us to involve one of our authors in every video segment that corresponds to material they address in the textbook. The involvement of the textbook authors is a very important part of this video package. One author introduces each of the 16 video segments, and brings a sense of expertise and immediacy to this ancillary.

Each video segment begins with an introduction by the textbook author who briefly discusses what follows and how it relates to the corresponding chapters in the textbook. Concept clues prior to the running video footage alert the viewer to vital information in the video. These are followed by approximately 10 minutes of running video that focuses on a subject corresponding to the textbook themes. Each video segment ends with a series of questions that take the viewer from video image to textbook concept. Text stills that foster critical thinking and stimulate concept recall appear behind the segment-ending questions.

Since the videos are designed to complement *Liberty, Equality, Power,* they are of the greatest value when used in conjunction with the textbook. This can be accomplished in a number of ways. Use the videos in the classroom, have your students view them at home, or both. Most students have access to a VCR, and the videos are inexpensive. When covering a chapter that corresponds to one of the video segments, assign the chapter and the video segment prior to your lecture. Then illustrate your lecture with the video, integrating it into your discussion and focusing on the subject as an illustration of the core concept. You can further utilize the video package by choosing some of the questions contained in this Instructor's Guide. Your use of the videos in the classroom and/or your posing questions about the video material in lectures or on exams encourages your students to use the videos at home.

The videos are also excellent lecture launchers. Prior to a lecture whose topic relates well to a certain video segment, you might wish to introduce the lecture with the video. Each video segment runs less than 15 minutes, leaving adequate lecture time. We have also had several class test sites in which the instructor has chosen to employ the video as a summation tool following a lecture. Both are very useful means of integrating the videos into the classroom. You might decide to make the videos available to your students on an optional basis by ordering copies for the bookstore or by placing your copy on reserve in the library. Whatever means you select, these videos, in tandem with *Liberty, Equality, Power* will give your students a greater understanding of the American experience.

This Guide provides you with information and suggestions for using the videos in the classroom. First, a brief Overview introduces the video topic and gives insights into the content of the video. This is followed by Classroom Use of Video Segments, which provides ideas for classroom discussion. The Concluding Questions section includes one or more essay test questions. Video to Text Issues focus on questions that tie together both *Liberty, Equality, Power* and the video segment. Selected Classroom Exercises are included for several video segments and suggest classroom or group projects. The Related Films section provides a brief list of films that elaborate on the topic covered in the video segment.

We believe that this unique video package serves as a marvelous teaching tool that helps bring American history to life. We offer this guide as a compass for using videos designed to directly complement a textbook. If, while using this video package along with *Liberty, Equality, Power,* you discover teaching strategies that enhance the classroom experience for your students, we welcome your ideas.

Access Codes to Videos

Volume I: America to 1877

When Old Worlds Collide
(access 00:00:43)

Slavery in New York City: Unearthing the Slave Trade
(access 00:14:36)

Newcomers to a New World: Contributions and Controversies
(access 00:27:18)

To Make This Land Prosper: Agriculture and Westward Settlement
(access 00:44:24)

Let the End Be Legitimate: The Supreme Court, The National Government, and The National Economy
(access 00:54:13)

Art, Romanticism, and Culture: Connections East and West
(access 01:19:37)

Constitutional Principles and Race Relations: The Beginning
(access 01:33:18)

Frederick Douglass: The Lesson of the Hour (I)
(access 01:59:17)

VOLUME I: AMERICA TO 1877
SUGGESTIONS FOR INSTRUCTIONAL USE OF VIDEO SEGMENTS CORRESPONDING TO CHAPTERS 1–6

WHEN OLD WORLDS COLLIDE

OVERVIEW

When Old Worlds Collide focuses on the theme of power as it describes Pre-Columbian Mesoamerica and the impact of the Spanish conquest on the Aztecs. The video segment concentrates on two primary topics; first, the pre-Aztec civilization at Teotihuacán, and, second, the story of the Spanish conquest of Mexico. The running video begins with views of modern Mexico City and then moves to clips ranging from the 1910 excavation of the Pyramid of the Sun at Teotihuacán to present work on the site. Archaeologists John Reece Davis and Esther Pastore describe the size and complexity of the pre-Aztec civilization. Both stress the power of ideology in building this vast civilization that had great influence on the later Aztecs. The remaining part of the excerpt tells the traditional story of the conquest of the Aztecs by Cortés and his small band of soldiers. Scenes from the Aztec Codex are used to illustrate this event, ending with the Spanish victory and the defeat of the Aztec nation.

CLASSROOM USE OF VIDEO SEGMENT

1. Discuss the surprising nature of the archaeological evidence found at Teotihuacán.
2. Focus on the degree of influence that Teotihuacán had on the Aztecs. Inquire about examples of earlier civilizations having significant effects on later cultures.
3. Discuss the power of myths and legends in making the Aztecs more vulnerable to conquest.

CONCLUDING QUESTIONS

1. The video makes only brief reference to the role of disease in the conquest of the Aztecs, yet we know, as the textbook points out, that the power of biological forces had a profound impact on the indigenous people of the Americas who had little resistance to the communicable diseases brought by the Europeans. Ask your class to draw from both video and textbook in order to explain the reasons why these commonplace European illnesses proved so devastating to the Aztecs as well as other Native Americans.
2. The power of religion proved essential in the swift conquest and pacification of the Americas. Have your students explain the reasons for this rapid conversion to Christianity and what elements were essential to this phenomenon.
3. Recent examination of the Spanish conquest of the Americas has questioned the role of traditional interpretations such as advanced technology or a more sophisticated socio-political organization. Have your students discuss the most recent interpretations of the role played by biological forces and by ideology and explain why these are more credible.

VIDEO TO TEXT ISSUES

1. Why was the experience of Cortés in Mexico different from that of Columbus in the Caribbean?
2. Compare and contrast the Spanish experience in Mexico with that of the Inca conquest in Peru.
3. What factors made the Spanish and English encounters in the Americas different?

SUGGESTED CLASSROOM EXERCISES

1. List examples of contemporary "cultural baggage" that originated from the European encounter/conquest of the Americas. What aspects are positive and which are negative?

RELATED FILMS

Columbus's World The second half of this initial film in the series "Columbus and the Age of Discovery" provides a good overview of Medieval Europe and explores the motivations for exploration in the fifteenth century.

The Sword and the Cross An excellent account of the impact of the conquistadors and the friars on the Mesoamerican cultures, offering new interpretations.

The Columbian Exchange A visual analysis of the effects of this phenomenon on modern life, this film enables the viewer to see the direct connection and influence of this pattern.

SLAVERY IN NEW YORK CITY: UNEARTHING THE SLAVE TRADE

OVERVIEW

The 1992 discovery of an African-American burial ground located in the heart of New York City opened up a new chapter in the city's history. Archaeologist Warren Barbour stresses how important this site is to understanding the role played by slaves in the development of colonial New York City. The city had the second largest slave population in the colonies and 40 percent of the city's total population was of African origin. Here we see a demonstration of the ambivalent relationship between liberty, equality, and power with slaves in colonial New York participating fully in urban life and helping to build the commercial base of the city. Bio-anthropologist Michael Blakey describes why slavery gave African Americans a unique history. Views of the port of Minna and an old slave fort on the African Gold Coast show the connections between the slave trade and the growth of prosperity in the Americas. Archaeologist Christopher DeCourse, an expert on the slave trade, explains why little is known about the African origins of those enslaved. The video ends with a commentary on slave life in colonial New York City, including the infamous 1712 slave revolt. Present-day excavation of the burial site promises to yield more information about the role of African Americans in building the largest city in this country.

CLASSROOM USE OF VIDEO SEGMENT

1. Have your class make a list of reasons why the New York City burial site is so important. Discuss each reason in class.

2. Discuss with your students why African migration to the Americas was so different from that of other groups. You might want to extend this exercise by focusing on the role of various aspects of power in creating these differences.

3. Have your students analyze the problems created by slaveholding during colonial times and how this form of power affected individuals' liberty and equality.

CONCLUDING QUESTIONS

1. This 1992 historical find resulted in the reopening of debate regarding the interpretation of roles played by African Americans in the colonial experience. Describe the insights provided by the work completed on this site.

2. The new evidence of slave life in colonial New York City uncovered at the burial site has provided material for diverse interpretations of the colonial period. Point out to your students how scholarly research continues to change our views of the past and then discuss what implications this holds for "conventional wisdom," traditional interpretations, and revisionist history.

VIDEO TO TEXT ISSUES

1. How are contemporary issues such as racism or power politics connected to new historical evidence such as this burial site?
2. In what ways can history be used or abused to support political views, social issues, or economic developments?

SUGGESTED CLASSROOM EXERCISES

1. Employ a pre-test to gauge knowledge and preconceptions about colonial slavery, especially as it related to the northern colonial urban environment. Use an open-ended post-test to measure reactions and change.

RELATED FILMS

"Origins" from *In Search of the Dream* An exploration of the impact of slavery on African-American life and culture from 1619 to the late twentieth century.

Digging for Slaves: The Excavation of American Slave Sites By describing three colonial slave-quarter sites, Middleburg Plantation, Monticello, and colonial Williamsburg, the viewer is given an accurate and surprising picture of slave life. The Monticello segment is especially useful for exploring racial attitudes that slavery engendered.

SUGGESTIONS FOR INSTRUCTIONAL USE OF VIDEO SEGMENTS CORRESPONDING TO CHAPTERS 7–12

NEWCOMERS TO A NEW WORLD: CONTRIBUTIONS AND CONTROVERSIES

OVERVIEW

Paul Johnson, the author of Chapters 7–12 of *Liberty, Equality, Power*, tells students how immigrants from Germany and Scandinavia moved to the West and established commercial market farming. This is also the primary focus of this video segment; the video coverage corresponds particularly well to sections in Chapter 9, Chapter 10, and Chapter 11. Both the video and Professor Johnson detail the transformation of the cities during the market revolution, and specifically point to the availability of cheap labor as a key to development. Both note the role of immigrants in developing urban sports, especially blood sports such as prize fighting. Finally, they explain the role immigrants played in the political and reform controversies of antebellum years. This includes examination of why the Whigs played to Nativists' fears, and how the issue of public schools and temperance became "immigrant" issues as well. The social effects of and response to immigrants are also covered well.

CLASSROOM USE OF VIDEO SEGMENT

1. Video and textbook point out that both appeals to change or resistance to change have often been cloaked in the language of liberty or equality, or the use of the threat of abusive power to scare citizens. Political parties have been using these tactics throughout our history, as have "reformers" and interest groups.

    a. Students can identify the political use of these appeals, and especially their use of the book's themes. Consider Federalists v. Jeffersonians, Democrats v. Whigs. For extension, instructors can have students carry this on through the rest of the course, right up to the alarmist and "patriotic" appeals heard today.

    b. Students can choose different reform movements (i.e., education, temperance, literacy, voting) and examine how movements use and misuse these themes. Be sure to have them make a similar examination of the arguments used by those "opposing reform."

    c. Have students consider special interest groups (bankers, monopolists, Nativists or others) and how they use these themes.

    d. Why would groups use these appeals, what legitimate concerns might they have for United States society, and why could they not see more than one side of the issues?

2. United States society changes in many ways, but does this always translate into better things for the American people?

    a. Rural society enters the market economy. Does this provide farmers and their families more power over their lives? Does it increase their equality vis-a-vis their neighbors, or increase their liberty and ability to advance further, or hurt them just as much?

    b. Cities grow as the nation becomes first commercialized and then industrialized. This increases the number of factory and industrial jobs available for men and women. Do these changes mean greater equality for all urban residents? Are they all empowered to the same extent? Have your students consider living quarters, political power, purchasing power, and distribution of income.

   c. For greater challenge and critical thinking, have students consider whether the new industrialists actually promoted "republican virtue" by developing the factory system (using the ideas of John Kasson) or if they instead were creating the horrors Melville depicted in "The Maids of Tartarus."

   d. You may also want your students to consider applying the video segment on farming to these ideas.

3. Racism, sexism, and greed all interfere with the acquisition of equality, liberty, or the distribution of power. Yet these are part of the human condition, and the history of the United States. Students should be able to identify how these issues interplayed with the themes of the textbook. They should also be able to trace their existence from the first days of the Republic to the present.

SUGGESTED CLASSROOM EXERCISES

1. For instructors who like comparative history, this segment allows comparisons between Old World and New. Consider how industrialism affected each continent, or how landownership laws affected the development of political systems.

2. This video segment can be used as a lead-in for urban history. Look at the changes brought by immigrant populations and rapidly growing urban populations. What were the conditions like in these cities? What city services that we take for granted were not available? How did slums develop?

3. Focus on family histories. This segment traces orally the lives of several immigrants. Students can be encouraged to go home and get oral history from family members, learning to personalize and apply United States history to themselves.

4. This video lets instructors start examining nativism, the fear of subversion, conspiracy theories, and scapegoating in United States history. This attitude can, unfortunately, be traced all the way to the present day. On a flip side, instructors could use this to begin a discussion of multiculturalism, and help students understand how diverse our national heritage is.

RELATED FILMS

Ethnic Notions One of the few videos available today on immigrants. This film deals with immigrant life and singularity, how this differed from the customs and traits of the established residents of the United States. It also touches on the nativist reaction to the apparent "clannishness" of the immigrants. Can be used to expand the study of immigrant life beyond the Irish.

Five Points Examines the legendary (or dreaded) Five Points district in New York City. This is where immigrants were herded, and from where other citizens claimed all lawlessness, disorder, and machine politics spewed forth. Another option from the detail on Boston is provided in the video clip. New York was the arrival location for the most immigrants, so using this video is very appropriate.

Beyond this, instructors can make use of three video indexes. The R. R. Bowker Company publishes two of them:

   a. The Educational Film & Video Locator of the Consortium of College and University Media Centers, two volumes.

   b. The AV Marketplace.

   c. Film and Video Finder, three volumes, by the National Information Center for Educational Media.

TO MAKE THIS LAND PROSPER: AGRICULTURE AND WESTWARD SETTLEMENT

OVERVIEW

Paul Johnson's textbook coverage links well with this video segment, in particular, early sections of Chapter 7, and Chapter 9, and throughout Chapter 12. There is marvelous treatment of the "Farmers Republic," households, work patterns, the social organization of communities and standards of living for rural areas. In addition, Johnson explains in the text how the natives are forced off their land to allow American farmers in. The text also makes the connection between Henry Clay's idea of regional agricultural specialization and the market economy. Detail is given on how the yeoman farmers in the Northeast and Old Northwest shift from self-sufficiency to becoming cogs in the free market economy. If you want to do something more, reinforce the connection between the Westward movement, agriculture, and the marketplace.

CLASSROOM USE OF VIDEO SEGMENT

1. Paul Johnson, in *Liberty, Equality, Power*, points out the importance of the agrarian republic lifestyle to the Founding Fathers. Key to this ideal were the twin features of property ownership and citizenship, along with the duties and responsibilities that come along with both to be a good citizen of the new nation. This provided for a well-ordered society where everyone knew their role. Instructors can:

    a. Note the connection between property and liberty. Have students extend the use of this ideal, and the duties (if any) still associated with this right up to the present day.

    b. Have your students consider that in this society equality and power were for white, male property owners only, and this meant powerlessness and inequality for everyone else. How can students justify this? Or have them explain how citizens then balanced this with the ideas of constitutional rights and a republican form of government.

    c. Consider using the power theme in the context that every major expansion across this continent was done in the name of providing more farmland for the "yeoman farmers" of the agrarian myth.

    d. Consider how rural society changed with the rise of the market economy. What does this mean for the future of the perfect "republican form of government" if the independent yeoman farmer just becomes a cog in the free market economy? What tensions could this cause in society?

    e. Use this video to demonstrate and connect the above issues.

2. The textbook provides considerable insight into the lives of women and children, how families worked, played, and struggled in both urban and rural communities. Their lives changed as the United States moved from a simple agrarian republic toward industrialism.

    a. What were the limits of liberty, power, and equality for women and children? Who or what determined these limits?

    b. Did any of these groups become more empowered as society changed? For example, how did women working in the Lowell Mills change their status in society?

    c. What steps did women take to improve their lives, their families, or society around them? How did these actions fit into the ideas of liberty, power, and equality?

    d. Videos on immigration and farming life both work with this to describe the lives of families in real terms and not just clichés.

SUGGESTED CLASSROOM EXERCISES

1. The Turner Frontier Thesis may be discussed with this video. How do its arguments seem true in this video, and what fallacies are obvious as well? This discussion may be extended to later times.

2. Note the yeoman farmer and the agrarian myth v. commercial free market economy. This myth continues today—just listen to members of the agriculture committees in Congress talk about farmers. Consider the role of the marketplace, transportation, machinery, etc. in the evolution of American agriculture.

3. What were the "good old days" really like? This is something that keeps coming up, with revivals and beliefs that things used to be better "back then." Use this as the first volley to discuss what life was really like. Ask students how many want to go back and live like these settlers did. Continue the same exposé up to the present.

RELATED FILMS

Gone West This is from Alistair Cooke's "America" series, which dates the material by some 20 years. It describes how the American people filled up the nation east of the Mississippi during the first half of the nineteenth century. It also includes information on the first migrations of settlers to the Pacific, conflicts with Native Americans, and how these encounters altered the cultures of both groups. Finally, it demonstrates the difficulties encountered by pioneers and settlers heading West, which connects nicely with the themes in both the video segment and the textbook.

America Grows Up Part I This video describes the transition of America from a rural and agricultural nation into an industrialized urban nation. It might not have enough on rural America for some instructors.

Life in America Around 1800 This is from the "Had You Lived Then" series. It focuses on daily life in a rural New England village. It lets students see how life could be tied to events in the general store and town hall. It also illustrates the growing connection to the market economy and democracy.

"The Expanding Nation" from the *American Adventure* series. This video connects the rapid growth of agriculture in the Old Northwest and Old Southwest with the expansion of industry in the antebellum United States. It also points out the geographic expansion west of the Mississippi and how the growth of a transportation network tied the nation together. Too ambitious for one video, but it has its moments.

"The Rural Republic" from the *American Adventure* series. It provides students with a clear picture of the ancient cycles of planting and harvesting as they existed in the rural world of the frontier. It examines social customs and rural order, how settlers formed communities and developed schools, courthouses, and legal order. Furthermore, it covers sexual divisions of labor in traditional America. This is an excellent match for material in *Liberty, Equality, Power.*

Beyond this you may utilize three excellent video indexes. The R. R. Bowker Company publishes two of them:

a. The Educational Film & Video Locator of the Consortium of College and University Media Centers, two volumes.

b. The AV Marketplace.

c. Film & Video Finder, three volumes, by the National Information Center for Educational Media.

If you want other ideas on how to raise questions about historical films, or get your students involved critiquing popular films based on historical topics, you can turn to two sources. The December 1986 issue of the *Journal of American History* and the December 1988 issue of the *American Historical Review* provide examples of both how historians question filmmaking accuracy and how they review the finished product.

LET THE END BE LEGITIMATE: THE SUPREME COURT, THE NATIONAL GOVERNMENT, AND THE NATIONAL ECONOMY

OVERVIEW

Liberty, Equality, Power, in Chapter 8, Chapter 9, and Chapter 11, as well as this video segment introduce students to the Supreme Court and the major cases of *Marbury* v. *Madison, McCulloch* v. *Maryland,* and *Gibbons* v. *Ogden.* The textbook raises the question about the role of the court in society and the idea of judicial review of cases. It also provides students a background about the role of the government in the economy. This debate starts with Hamilton and Jefferson, is carried through Henry Clay and the American System, and the issue of government spending and intervention as applied to canals, tariffs, etc. The debate about the government's role in economic development continues into the Jacksonian period with Jackson v. the Whigs. What is the role of the government in a market economy? Should it stay out entirely, or does it have a responsibility to promote economic development, thus increasing power and equality for all? How this debate applied to banking powers, international relations, and court rulings are all examined by text and video. In addition, the text provides marvelous information in the rest of Chapter 9 on the conversion from agrarianism to industrialism, and how this affects people. This, of course, has a direct relationship to citizens' views on the government's role in the economy.

CLASSROOM USE OF VIDEO SEGMENT

1. This all ties into the video segment quite well. You can use this reading material as an introduction, or remind students that nothing occurs in a vacuum. Political issues, social issues, economic issues, and legal decisions are all linked and influence each other.

2. You might want to remind students (either on their own or referring them back to earlier chapters in the book) that there was a need for the Commerce Clause and federal regulation of trade. Consider the economic warfare between states during the Confederation period (1781–1787), and they will better understand Chief Justice Marshall's determination that the national government's power over commerce be strong. Also focus on the relationship between the federal power under the Commerce Clause and the regulation of slavery. Students might not understand Southerners' insistence that federal power be limited in banking unless they understand its implication for slavery. A consideration of South Carolina's paranoia about its slaves might be advantageous here (along the lines of William Freehling's books). You could carry this debate over government power and regulation right up to the present, including evidence showing where self-interest is cloaked in terms of "states' rights."

3. The Founding Fathers' liberty increased with a limited central government. This part of the textbook hotly debates this idea and the role of government changes. The debate is still going on today, with arguments over how much the national, state, or local governments should regulate the economy, morality, etc. Have your students start a timeline and trace the roots of current arguments from the earliest days of our constitutional government.

    a. At the most basic level, students can identify how the role of the government changes between 1790 and 1860, and why.

    b. Students should identify the connection between social issues and government action, and the reasons advocated for or against government intervention. They can tie this into the struggle between liberty and power.

    c. Students should do the same thing for economic issues, and examine the myth of laissez faire.

    d. There is an ongoing struggle for power between the national and state governments. (This can also be traced from Confederation days to current welfare and other reform arguments.) Have students think critically about this struggle—is it another example of the struggle between liberty and power? Are the two always mutually exclusive? How do citizens come out the winner, and what promotes equality?

e. How do students explain the rise of political parties using the debate over liberty and power, and questions about the role of government? Students can trace the development of Federalists, Democratic-Republicans, Whigs, and other parties—and their ideologies—to the present-day parties. How have the basic appeals and definitions of liberty, equality, and power changed as society changes?

f. Our government evolved from a deferential representative republican government to a democracy during this time period. But it became a democracy for whom? How much liberty, power, and equality did the people gain, and was this equally divided? Who was left out of the loop, and how did the rest of the citizens and leaders justify this with our constitutional principles? (Another line of reasoning that students can continue throughout the course.)

g. The video on immigration also applies to this topic.

4. *Liberty, Equality, Power* also examines foreign relations as an issue of liberty and power. Using this idea, students can investigate our foreign relations and wars.

a. How do these events increase or decrease our power and liberty as a nation? What was the intent of the actions on our part?

b. How does the outcome of our foreign relations increase liberty, equality, or power for the average citizen?

c. The beginning of Chapter 9 provides a great link between foreign affairs and domestic legislation.

SUGGESTED CLASSROOM EXERCISES

1. History of the Supreme Court and the Constitution. This can be connected with background of the Founding Fathers, the Federalist Papers, and their intent for both the Constitution and the Court's role in government. This history could include how the role and the views of the Court vary depending on its composition and the current attitudes in American society. Use the examples of the Taney Court and the Dred Scott decision, the conservative bastions of the 1920s and the changes in the 1930s, and up through the Warren and Rehnquist courts.

2. Use the video to discuss the ongoing struggle between power and liberty, and over who shall exercise both. This can be linked to changing economic ideas and prosperity, to the argument between state v. national powers, or to the question about personal rights and liberties. Another possibility is to consider the issue of personal v. corporate rights, or the public good v. private property rights. All are introduced in this video segment.

3. The role of government, from early republic to the present. Why should the national government be powerful, and do we still need this today? How powerful is too powerful; i.e., when does the exercise of power become an abuse? Trace the extension of regulatory power from these cases to the Interstate Commerce Commission in 1887, the Food and Drug Administration, OSHA, and others today. What is the real issue behind the power to tax, or to create and control the money supply? Why is it constitutional to create national banks, but not the Federal Reserve as some groups suggest? When is regulation considered to be for the public good, and how can you determine this? (Consider *Munn* v. *Illinois* and other cases as an extension.)

4. What is the correct interpretation of the Constitution and its grants of power? What is meant by "original intent" of the writers of the document and its amendments, and how do you apply that then and now? What is the difference between "strict construction" and a loose interpretation of the Constitution, and why are each important? This can be used to delve into the issues of judicial review, civil rights legislation, affirmative action, gun control, personal privacy laws (i.e., abortion) and the claim that government should impose religion and morality.

RELATED FILMS

John Marshall: Profile in Courage This is a biographical look at Marshall and his career. It is not very impartial, and defends him and his decisions against any charges of partisanship. However, it does accurately portray his determination to strengthen national power and the Constitution v. the states, and thus help the nation survive.

Equal Justice Under Law: Marbury v. Madison This is the first video in the series the students view for this segment. This video covers the Marshall Court's affirming the right of judicial review by the Supreme Court. The dramatization reminds everyone that law evolves from real-life events.

Beyond this you can make use of three excellent video indexes. The R. R. Bowker Company publishes two of them:

a. The Educational Film & Video Locator of the Consortium of College and University Media Centers, two volumes.

b. The AV Marketplace.

c. Film and Video Finder, three volumes, by the National Information Center for Educational Media.

If you want other ideas on how to raise questions about historical films, and how to get your students involved critiquing popular films based on historical topics, you can turn to two sources. The December 1986 issue of the *Journal of American History* and the December 1988 issue of the *American Historical Review* provide examples of both how historians question filmmaking accuracy and how they review the finished product.

ART, ROMANTICISM, AND CULTURE: CONNECTIONS EAST AND WEST

OVERVIEW

Chapters 10 and 12 take a close look at the development of American popular culture. The author includes a look at literature, the rise of "sentimentality" in writing, and the fine arts. He establishes for the students the unique relationship between the wilderness frontier and American civilization. This was understood (even overemphasized) by generations of artists and writers. The wilderness provides the difference between what is European or American, between Old World and New. The author also introduces the artists' belief in the morality and godliness of nature, and explains that some persons were already questioning whether man and nature could coexist, but were sure that humanity could learn lessons from nature if it paid attention. Note the role of Niagara Falls in the East as an example. The textbook, combined with this video segment, provides a clear basis for Eastern art and its appreciation of the West.

CLASSROOM USE OF VIDEO SEGMENT

1. Stress to your students the connection between the ideas of artists and what they saw (or expected to see) in the West. Are the artists' assumptions correct? Do they reinforce the ideas held by Cole and Easterners about the connection between nature and Native Americans, that those who live closest to nature learn the most from it?

2. You might want to provide more information about Thomas Cole and the Hudson River school of artists. Slides of Cole's work, along with that of Inness or Bingham, would also help.

3. The United States develops its own culture—literature, art forms, entertainment. Each of these reflects the democratic impulse of the nation in some way.

   a. What causes the development of popular literature, and how does it reflect or even promote the themes of liberty and equality?

© 2002 Thomson Learning, Inc.

b. Changes in popular sports emerge in the cities—are they a sign of power shifts, or greater liberty?

c. How does the evolution of America's artists reflect the ideas of liberty, of religion and morality, and of the belief in America's unique place in the world?

d. Even the shifts in the educational system, or the promotion of widespread education, reflect a belief that this will give power and equality to some citizens. How is this so?

SUGGESTED CLASSROOM EXERCISES

1. You may use this video to raise environmental issues; how environmentally conscious have Americans been throughout history? What is the effect of "civilization" on nature? The pictures of Bodner along the Missouri River and out West make a nice counter-play to images of strip mining, deforestation, etc. Can nature and industry coexist without injuring each other? George Inness suggests they can; events in Oregon and elsewhere argue otherwise.

2. Examine cultural exchanges and diversity in the American past. You can also link the past to the present here. What has the effect of disease been on other cultures we have encountered? (Both in the past and currently.) This ties into examination of the treatment of Native Americans, their poverty and policies toward them, from colonial through the present.

3. This video could be used as part of an examination of Native Americans and their culture.

4. Also appropriate is a discussion of popular myths and images of the American West, both from the eyes of Easterners and from Europe.

RELATED FILMS

Views of a Vanishing Frontier This video concentrates on the travels of Karl Bodner, one of the three artists examined in the video segment. In many ways it is an extended version of what the segment does, because it documents their travels from 1832–1833 up the Missouri River, re-creates the lives of Native Americans before they are struck down with white diseases, and views the frontier before it is assaulted environmentally. The details of Native American dress and ceremonies are striking.

SUGGESTIONS FOR INSTRUCTIONAL USE OF VIDEO SEGMENTS CORRESPONDING TO CHAPTERS 13–19

CONSTITUTIONAL PRINCIPLES AND RACE RELATIONS: THE BEGINNING

OVERVIEW

This video segment addresses the question of the compromises on slavery that emerged in discussions during the Constitutional Convention. It also speaks to the relation of these compromises to the practical but paradoxical determination among the men gathered in Philadelphia to protect individual liberty, security, and property while at the same time establishing a government that could not be torn apart by faction or passion. Bill Moyers, in this video originally produced for the bicentennial of the Constitutional Convention, talks with three historians, Michael Kammen of Cornell University, Forrest McDonald of the University of Alabama, and Olive Taylor of Howard University.

In the initial segment, Moyers questions Forrest McDonald on the value systems of the Founding Fathers vis-a-vis their willingness to compromise on the slavery question in order to succeed in creating a national government that could govern effectively. McDonald notes that protecting liberty was of primary importance to the framers and that the protection of liberties could not occur without union. To have a union, he argues, the framers had to recognize practical realities. He points to the 3/5 compromise as a primary example.

The second part of this segment focuses on Moyers' interview with Olive Taylor, whose most recent scholarly work examines Chief Justice of the Supreme Court John Marshall, "Mr. Constitution." She explains that her interest in Justice Marshall emanated from his insistence on protecting property rights during his tenure on the Court. As a result of this determination and his interest in promoting the sovereignty of the national government, Marshall's decisions even overrode state efforts to loosen the bonds of slavery. To Moyers' question regarding Marshall's racial views, Taylor iterates that the chief justice's position on the issue of slavery in the states had nothing to do with race hatred. She believes that he saw the United States as a "beacon for white people" and a symbol for the realization (ironically) of man's desire for freedom and self-determination. To John Marshall and many like him, blacks simply had no place in this worldview.

Although highly critical of the Founding Fathers and shapers of history like John Marshall, Taylor recognizes that the reality of nineteenth-century belief in the sanctity of property and the heritage of Anglo-Saxon jurisprudence meant that these men were not going to tamper with the institution of slavery. She uses the carving of the nation's capital out of two slave states to illustrate their willingness to compromise on the issue of slavery, in part to pacify southerners concerned about antislavery agitation in New York and Pennsylvania and to win Southern support for Alexander Hamilton's economic policy.

Despite such practical, if unfortunate, considerations, Taylor admits that the genius of the document is that it can be changed and that the Constitution has a positive meaning for most blacks. Although it took many years, "the moral arm of the universe" did bend toward justice—as evidenced in the Constitution's ability to finally bring justice to the doorstep of all Americans, regardless of race. The Constitution lives, she concludes, and it works.

In the video segment's final part, Moyers interviews Michael Kammen. Moyers relates Carl Sandburg's statement that Lincoln said yes to the Constitution when it could be a help and no when it became a hindrance. Kammen contends that the Constitution is a living document that fortunately allows the kind of flexibility that Lincoln demonstrated. During the Civil War, America's single greatest crisis as a people, the question "Is the Constitution adequate to a crisis like this?" constantly arose. The outcome proved it was. It also revealed that the Constitution could serve as a means to an end—the preservation of our individual rights, security, and the cohesion of a nation.

CLASSROOM USE OF VIDEO SEGMENT

1. First list and then discuss the values involved in the treatment of the issue of slavery at the Constitutional Convention.

2. Have your students reflect on John Marshall's interpretation of the Constitution as it relates to the questions of African Americans and the issues of liberty, equality, and power.

3. The video segment refers to the "genius" of the Constitution. Have your class analyze this claim, in particular, as related to race relations.

4. Discuss how Abraham Lincoln reflected that "genius" in his presidency.

CONCLUDING QUESTIONS

1. Although Chief Justice John Marshall adhered to the principle of the sanctity of property rights that allowed the institution of slavery to remain viable, he also asserted the supremacy of the national government over the states in his decisions. How did the precedents set in Marshall's decisions ultimately serve the purposes of those who opposed slavery?

2. In terms of the institution of slavery and black civil rights, how did the "moral arm of justice" bend during the decade preceding the Civil War and through the Reconstruction era? What made this possible at that time and again some one hundred years later?

3. "Free Soil" advocates denounced the Dred Scott decision as a "gross perversion" of the Constitution, while southerners gloated that "Southern opinion upon the subject of Southern slavery . . . is now the supreme law of the land." What constitutional debate in the post–Mexican War era did these opposing positions reflect? What did this dispute say about the document the framers of the Constitution produced?

4. Carl Sandburg said that Abraham Lincoln said yes to the Constitution when it was a help and no when it was a hindrance. How is Lincoln's practical genius in using the Constitution reflected in his actions in the events immediately preceding the outbreak of the Civil War and in decisions he made during the war and as the war drew to a close?

VIDEO TO TEXT ISSUES

1. Did Americans not see the hypocrisy and paradox inherent in the compromises on the issue of slavery in the Constitution? Explain.

2. If the framers of the Constitution and subsequent eras could compromise on the issue of slavery, why was this not possible in the decade preceding the Civil War?

SUGGESTED CLASSROOM EXERCISES

1. Since the constitutional debates that preceded the Civil War are among the most important in American history, this video segment and the one that follows offer an excellent launching point for an examination of constitutional issues reflected in the

   a. post–Mexican War debate over slavery in the territory acquired from Mexico.

   b. appearance of a Free Soil Party.

   c. forging of the Compromise of 1850.

   d. Lincoln–Douglas debates.

   e. Kansas crisis.

   f. Dred Scott and other Supreme Court decisions in the period.

   g.   position Lincoln's assumption on the nature of the Southern rebellion and the president's role in responding to it, his decision to issue the Emancipation Proclamation, his conduct of the war, and his view of reconstructing the South.

   h.   debate between Congress and the president (Lincoln and Johnson) on plans of Reconstruction.

   i.   passage of civil rights legislation during the Reconstruction period and the de facto abrogation of black civil rights by the end of the nineteenth century.

2.   The subject of conflicting interpretations of the Constitution relating to a variety of issues today is a relevant topic that students can easily discuss and for which they can find many current examples. [Debates over gun control, affirmative action, the extent of the federal government's obligation to provide for the general welfare, a citizen's privacy versus the government's responsibility to regulate (abortion), and legislation that abridges individual liberty for the common good (prohibitions against smoking in public places, for example).]

3.   These video segments also can be used as a basis for critical thinking exercises that demand the analysis of historical data to reach an appropriate conclusion or to explain a decision or an action.

   a.   To address the constitutional issues inherent in the Dred Scott decision and the significance of the context in which the justices heard the case, distribute the basic elements of the arguments in Taney's opinion, as well as a descriptive composite of each justice sitting on the Supreme Court at the time the Dred Scott case reached the court and a description of the context in which the decision was handed down—controversial events that had preceded the hearing of the case. Ask students to draw conclusions based on an analysis of this data and to explain how this decision was a product of its time, much as the compromises on slavery in the Constitutional Convention reflected the pressure of the job at hand and the times in which the framers lived.

   b.   An analysis of events in the aftermath of the Mexican War that led to the Kansas crisis offers the opportunity to understand how the effort to compromise generated more problems than it solved.

   c.   An examination of the behavior of Southern secessionists, abolitionists, and Radical Republicans reflects the consequences of a refusal to compromise on constitutional principles or to accept the legitimacy of the Constitution in a crisis (in the case of the "Fire Eaters" and the William Lloyd Garrison brand of abolitionism).

RELATED FILMS

The Sellin' of Jamie Thomas, Parts 1 and 2 A dramatization of the sale of a slave family, their escape to freedom, and the threat of bounty hunters to that freedom.

Digging for Slaves: The Excavation of American Slave Sites An examination of three slave quarter excavations at eighteenth-century sites at Monticello, Williamsburg, and Middleburg Plantation that contribute to our knowledge of the reality of slavery.

In Search of the Dream: Origins A review of the origins of slavery in seventeenth-century Virginia, the impact of the institution on African Americans, and the African cultural heritage still reflected in American life.

Uncle Tom's Cabin A description of the impact of Harriet Beecher Stowe's novel and the popularity of the play that was produced across the United States in the post–Civil War period concluding with an abridged dramatic production of the play.

FREDERICK DOUGLASS: THE LESSON OF THE HOUR (I)

OVERVIEW

In this final video segment on Volume I, actor Fred Morsell dramatizes the last and most important speech delivered by Frederick Douglass. Titled "The Lesson of the Hour," this speech reflects the horror and disgust famed runaway slave and abolitionist leader Douglass felt as Southern whites used lynchings and economic, political, and social degradation to return blacks to a virtual enslaved condition in the late nineteenth century. He eloquently appeals to Americans to uphold the basic principles on which their nation was built. Only then, he argues, could justice prevail for all the people. Chapter 18 in *Liberty, Equality, Power* provides a very nice complement to this video segment. You might wish to have your students read the chapter and then follow with Douglass' speech at the end of class or have the students view it on their own after reading the chapter and essay.

CLASSROOM USE OF VIDEO SEGMENT

1. Describe and analyze Douglass' solutions to the "Negro problem."
2. According to Morsell's depiction of Douglass, describe Douglass' frame of mind when he wrote and delivered this speech.

CONCLUDING QUESTIONS

1. To what post–Civil War outrages against blacks was Douglass referring and what effect did this have on his perception of the importance of this speech? Did his speech accomplish what he hoped?

SUGGESTED CLASSROOM EXERCISES

1. An analysis of how and why, after a Civil War and traumatic post-war period, African Americans failed to experience the full protection of their rights under the Constitution.

For "Text to Video Issues" and "Related Films," see the previous video segment.

NOTES

NOTES

NOTES

NOTES

NOTES

NOTES

NOTES

NOTES

NOTES

NOTES

NOTES